THE Bluffer's Guide to FOOD

Neil Davey

Hammersley House
5-8 Warwick Street
London W1B 5LX
United Kingdom

Email: info@bluffers.com
Website: bluffers.com
Twitter: @BluffersGuide

Published 2014

Publisher: Thomas Drewry
Publishing Director: Brooke McDonald

Series Editor: David Allsop
Design and Illustration: Jim Shannon

A CIP Catalogue record for this book is available from the British Library.

ISBN: 978-1-909937-12-3 (print)
978-1-909937-13-0 (ePub)
978-1-909937-14-7 (Kindle)

CONTENTS

You can't even take shelter in a library because there's a very good chance it will now be the site of a Malaysian/ Persian hybrid pop-up restaurant.

...TO START

Food is everywhere in the Western world, which is just as well because we wouldn't last long without it. But now it has gone far beyond its primary role as essential sustenance to become a central part of modern culture. These days it's impossible to turn on the TV without stumbling across someone demonstrating a recipe, someone else screaming profanities about another's culinary skills, or a large American man attempting to devour a hamburger the size of a small child.

And it's not just TV. You can't pick up a newspaper or magazine without finding a celebrity telling you how to cook, a chef telling you how to eat or a supplement featuring a celebrity chef doing both. Pubs are becoming gastropubs, street vendors are opening restaurants and trained chefs are taking to the street. You can't even take shelter in a library because there's a very good chance it will now be the site of a Malaysian/Persian hybrid pop-up restaurant, a supper club or the location for a post-ironic tweed-clad street food collective's 'twist' on the Wimpy burger.

Even sitting down to dinner with friends won't help. As you eat, conversations frequently turn to recollections of great meals you've had, where you've eaten recently, and what you've cooked this week. At the same time, you will be expected to analyse every bite of the food on your plate, listen to a detailed explanation of the cooking techniques involved and the precise sources of each individual ingredient, *and* plan where you should go for brunch tomorrow.

The rules have changed. It's no longer enough to be a food lover who once attempted something Keith Floyd cooked on TV. Now you have to be a food worshipper with a wealth of experience under your belt, a desire to analyse (and photograph) everything you consume ('I know it looks like a slice of cheddar and a cream cracker, but it's a "deconstructed, scallion-drop, rustic cheese biscuit"') and a depth of knowledge that could win you Mastermind. ('And your specialist subject?' 'Obscure world cuisine, 1800 to the present day.')

The subject of food is increasingly a minefield where, in order to survive with your credibility intact, you will be expected to know exactly what's being talked about when your dinner companions are discussing the relative merits of *bo ssam* and *warabi-mochi* – or Korean pork in a lettuce leaf and a Japanese pudding made with bracken starch, if you prefer.

The days of just sitting back and having a pleasantly relaxed dinner are long gone. Food is to be studied and dissected as much as it is masticated and tasted. If that sounds like too much hard work, you're right. And that's why this book exists.

You may wonder why the term 'food worshipper' is to be preferred to the ubiquitous 'foodie'. The fact is that the people who get described as 'foodies' loathe the word. The use of the term thus shows you up as a non-foodie, which is not the food bluffer's objective.

'Food worshipper' suggests a level of cult devotion entirely appropriate to the world of food.

What better description might there be for these extreme lovers of food? Good question. So far, at the time of publication, no single universally adopted term has yet emerged. 'Food connoisseur' is a bit pompous; 'food lover' is perfectly acceptable, although it does leave the door open for jokes about inappropriate behaviour with chocolate eclairs. For the bluffer, however, 'connoisseur' and 'lover' don't quite cover the level of obsession you are about to encounter. 'Food worshipper', on the other hand, suggests a level of cult devotion entirely appropriate to the world of food.

You must also be loath to use the word 'passion'. It is something you will hear a lot in food-based conversations, and must be avoided at all costs. You must never say, for example, 'It's so lovely to meet an artisan producer who's so passionate about what they do' or 'so passionate about the welfare of their animals' or 'so passionate' about every other tiny aspect of their food business. If you want to eulogise about an artisan baker who is 'passionate' about using only organic rice paper from a Vietnamese workers' cooperative, then think of another word. 'Zealous' or 'enthusiastic' are good ones.

This is a fascinating and often complex world you are about to immerse yourself in, but, with the right guidance, your talent, and a grasp of facial expressions ranging from piety to insouciance, you're going to be fine. This short but definitive guide will conduct you through the main danger zones encountered in discussions about food, and equip you with a vocabulary and evasive technique that will minimise the risk of being rumbled as a bluffer. It will give you a few easily remembered nuggets of essential information that might even allow you to be accepted as a food expert of rare ability and experience. But it will do more. It will give you the tools to impress legions of marvelling listeners with your forensic knowledge of the subject – without anyone discovering that, until you read it, you didn't know the difference between the *sous vide* method and the Maillard reaction.

Ladies and gentlemen. Bluffing is served…

FOOD FOR THOUGHT

The Cambridge World History of Food runs to several thousand pages and two shelf-threatening volumes. This chapter is going to attempt to cover much the same ground in approximately one-eleventh of a Bluffer's Guide. It's a big task and one that is, frankly, unlikely to be easily accomplished.

However, don't lose heart. You will be relieved to discover that a comprehensive knowledge of food is not the bluffer's way. Instead, your cunning strategy is to be armed with the salient points, to avoid too many questions and to be able to bring a conversation back to the subjects you do know.

The downside of the subject matter is its breadth. The advantage, therefore, is also its breadth. There is no shame in admitting that you don't know everything about food (How can you possibly know everything when there are so many world cuisines and so many regional variations within them?), provided that you know enough – or can bluff enough – around the gaps in your knowledge.

THE HUMILITY RUSE

There are points to be scored by accepting your limitations. The irony of this particular *Bluffer's Guide* is that it is preparing you to go up against food worshippers who, in around 90% of cases, are also bluffing. It might be to a lesser extent, it might be to a greater extent, but take it as gospel: the overwhelming majority of people who claim to know about food are bluffing.

Take the person who's a self-proclaimed expert on Japanese food. No, they are not. They may believe they are, but they are wrong. How can this be stated with such confidence? Because the famous Japanese chef Nobu Matsuhisa does not consider himself to be a sushi expert. The average sushi chef will spend the first year or two of their career cooking nothing but rice. They are not allowed anywhere near a piece of seaweed, let alone a piece of fish or a sharp knife, for months – in some cases years. This process instils a degree of humility, which is why a man in the fifth decade of his career and who owns 25 Japanese restaurants worldwide still thinks he's a sushi novice. And that's why it can be said that someone who's looked up sushi online, picked a plate of *sashimi* off a conveyor belt, and once bought a pack of cellophane-wrapped fish and rice from a cold cabinet is not an expert.

Sushi chefs, however, can teach the bluffer a great deal, as a similar degree of humility is a useful weapon in the bluffing arsenal that, genuine or practised, will make you more credible. Unless the person you are jousting with is a professional restaurant critic or chef (*and* has accumulated half-a-million air miles eating around the globe), it's a near 100% certainty that they will be bluffing about at least some aspect of the food they are discussing. The seasoned bluffer – in other words, anyone with this book at his or her disposal – can assume an attitude of supreme nonchalance and cheerfully admit his or her shortcomings over certain cuisines. In a world where bluffing is the norm, it is perhaps those quietly candid moments that are the most powerful. They show a sense of modesty, a willingness to learn about new things, and permit one to make statements such as: 'Well, that's the thing with food – you can't know everything, and it's the journey of discovery that I enjoy the most.' And then, of course, you will gently steer the conversation back to the food-related subjects with which you are the most familiar.

IS IT AUTHENTIC?

You will also find one word cropping up at very regular intervals: 'authenticity'. It is, it seems, every food worshipper's *raison d'être* to find the most 'authentic' experience they can. Whenever you go to an ethnic restaurant of any description, the first question you'll be asked, even before 'Was it any good?' or 'Did you like it?' will be, 'Was it authentic?' This is a very good thing; rarely has there been a question that serves as a finer opening gambit for bluffers.

Many lesser food-worshipping types would panic at the question. At its heart it seems to ask how well-travelled you are and how able you are to recall individual dishes consumed on those travels. It also presumes, of course, that what you tried on those travels were quintessential examples of the dishes in question (and they probably weren't). The assumption, therefore, is that if you haven't travelled and if your vocabulary, memory and taste buds do not work closely in sync, your opinion is of lesser importance. This is nonsense. The question of 'authenticity' is actually the perfect opportunity to demonstrate a small but perfect knowledge of food history and, should you require, deflect attention from your own experiences or lack of them.

Let's take a few famous dishes as examples.

THE CLASSIC AMERICAN HAMBURGER

The clue is in the name. The original meat patty was a German sausage named after the city of Hamburg (the Frankfurter would be another good example, of course). As it happens, what we now know as the hamburger – a small patty of minced beef – existed before the Germans claimed to have invented it; there are ancient Italian and Russian versions, to name but two. However, when German sailors emigrated to the USA taking their small beefy cakes with them, the 'hamburger' name stuck. So when someone asks you if the hamburger you ate the other day was 'authentic', you can smile knowingly and begin a short lecture in food history and geography. Or declare it to be as authentically American as apple pie – because that probably originated with the Dutch and then came over to the USA from England with the Pilgrim Fathers.

SPAGHETTI BOLOGNESE

In Bologna, the pasta most commonly eaten is tagliatelle or lasagne. Their meat sauces use hearty chunks of meat simmered down into something known as *ragù alla bolognese.* Accordingly, spaghetti is not a pasta particularly associated with Bologna. The 'authenticity' question in relation to spag bol is therefore a bluffer's gift. It should, strictly speaking, be a tag bol.

If you want to talk 'authentic' Italian, you're probably looking at the sort of feasts Nero is said to have enjoyed: sculpted pork statues, stuffed womb of sow and food eaten off naked women. (Interestingly enough, this practice, known as *nyotaimori,* lives on to this day in Japan. See how that one plays out at your local trattoria or branch of Pizza Express.)

TEMPURA

Tempura refers to little slices of fish or pieces of vegetables served in a coating of the lightest, airiest, most delicate batter known to man. With the possible exception of *sushi* and *sashimi,* few things scream Japanese cuisine more than a piece of tempura. You can guess what's coming, of course… In fact, tempura is Portuguese in origin and probably arrived in Japan via Portuguese missionaries in the sixteenth century. So, was that tempura course you enjoyed the other night authentic? No, of course it wasn't; it was Portuguese food in a Japanese restaurant.

INDIAN FAVOURITES

It is widely known that chicken tikka masala isn't actually Indian in origin. The tikka bit is Indian (*tikka*, by the way, apparently translates as 'bits') but the 'masala' element originated in Scotland. As the story goes, at some point in the 1970s a customer at Glasgow's Shish Mahal restaurant complained that his chicken was too dry, so chef Ali Ahmed Aslam rustled up a sauce – a 'masala gravy' – made with a few spices and a tin of condensed tomato soup that he had to hand. The rest is, as they say…

That means, of course, that if you want an authentic experience in an Indian restaurant, you'll have to pick something much more traditional, like a vindaloo. Only that's also Portuguese: *carne de vinha d'alhos*, a dish of meat with wine (*vinha*) and garlic (*alho*). In the Indian version, wine becomes vinegar and there are more spices and aromatic ingredients than just garlic, but it's still based on a European original. And we'll come to the spices in due course…

(Ironically, chicken tikka masala has made it back to the Indian subcontinent, so you could find a restaurant serving it and order a portion, in which case you can be in India eating a genuinely 'authentic' Scottish meal.)

FISH AND CHIPS

It surely doesn't get more authentically British than fish and chips. There's a great sense of nostalgia – genuine or otherwise – towards the original and perennial fast food. Nothing says Great British tradition like cod and chips out of a newspaper on the seafront, vinegar dripping from your fingers, a pickled onion resting on the side.

Only – as you've no doubt realised – fried fish is Portuguese. Again. In the seventeenth century, Jewish refugees from Portugal introduced deep-fried fish – *peixe frito* – to Britain. You can also argue, of course, that potatoes aren't authentically British, as we didn't get them until the sixteenth century, when Sir Walter Raleigh or Sir Francis Drake brought them over from the Americas, depending on which version of the tale you believe.

If 'authentic' means food that's indigenous to a nation, then the Brits should be eating moles and badgers.

You might see now why the 'authenticity' question is manna from heaven for the bluffer. It boils down to one simple element: where – or, more accurately, when – does one draw the line? If 'authentic' means food that's indigenous to a nation, then the Brits should be eating moles and badgers. Pasta in a tomato-based sauce wouldn't exist in Italy, as tomatoes originated in South America and didn't get introduced to Europe until around the sixteenth century. India would be eating much blander food if it weren't for the Portuguese (naturally), who introduced them to the chilli pepper.

On that note, the Spice Route is a marvellous bit of food history with which to demonstrate your superior (if limited) knowledge. It also explains how the Portuguese became such a power in the food world, even if it was only for a very short time.

HOT AND SPICY

In a nutshell, the Spice Route refers to the trade lines between the key historic civilisations of Asia, Africa and Europe. It was this trading that saw spices such as cinnamon, ginger and cardamom spread from their origins and pop up in various bits of world cuisine. They're also the reason that chillies – ostensibly originating in Central and South America – spread to Asia.

Trade in spices started well before the beginning of the Christian era in the Middle East, pretty much the busiest point for overland caravans (in their original sense, rather than the one in front of you on a single carriageway). As various forces became more powerful – for example, Islam and the Ottoman Empire – overland routes started to close, pushing people in different directions and aiding the growth of the sea routes.

By the fifteenth century, Muslim traders dominated the sea trade throughout the Indian Ocean, shipping spices from sources in the Far East and India to the Persian Gulf and Red Sea and then overland into Europe. So, in order to avoid the high taxes being charged by the Ottoman Empire who now controlled the routes, Europe looked for an alternative. Thanks to Portuguese explorer Vasco da

Gama, they found one. In 1498, da Gama pioneered the Europe to Indian Ocean route via Africa, sailing around the Cape of Good Hope.

There is, of course, rather more to it than that, but this is a food guide, not a history lecture. There's lots of good information about the Spice Route out there, but the basics should be enough to back up your points. Trading has been going on for centuries (which is why even Tudor recipes include ingredients such as mace and nutmeg), politics have forced assorted changes, and we have all pretty much benefited from the hybrid cuisines that have resulted. The other key benefit is the easy dismissiveness with which you can now deflate the 'authenticity' argument. After all, what is the cut-off point? When does a dish 'belong' to a particular country rather than being an amalgamation of ingredients that were never indigenous in the first place?

In the case of chilli peppers and Asia, the former are a relatively recent introduction courtesy of Christopher Columbus who first brought them back to Europe from Central and South America, and the Portuguese traders who took them further east. And, very possibly, other traders then took them from India to Eastern Europe and Turkey and then to Hungary: how else do you think paprika became a key ingredient of goulash?

On the subject of travels and food, there is a long-held belief that Marco Polo introduced pasta into Italy after seeing the noodle in China. Happily, in bluffing terms, this theory holds as much weight as the famous April Fool about spaghetti growing on trees.

The most likely explanation is that Arab invaders introduced a dried noodle-like foodstuff to Sicily in the eighth century. (There is also evidence that a durum wheat noodle existed in the region as early as the first century, although it was baked rather than boiled.) Pasta, you may wish to note for pontification purposes, translates as 'dough' or 'paste', and shares the same root as 'pâté' and 'pastry'.

SPREAD OF THE SPUD

And while on the subject of carbohydrates, this seems a good time to look at the potato. As Asia got the chilli, Europe got the humble spud. Peru is where the potato originated and the country still grows some 4,000 varieties. Although it was around the mid-sixteenth century that the British Isles first came across this vegetable, potatoes weren't eaten in any great number until 200 years later. Now, of course, it's hard to keep up with demand.

Initially, the potato wasn't too popular. Indeed, when Prussia suffered famine in 1744, King Frederick the Great had to order his people to consume them. In England, their connection to Spain had eighteenth-century farmers denouncing potatoes as a Roman Catholic threat, and France was not too keen on them either. And then, in the late eighteenth century, along came Antoine-Augustin Parmentier.

As you'd expect from someone who gave his name to a potato dish, he was a bit of a fan. Legend has it that, as a rather inept soldier (how else do you describe someone captured by the Prussians five times in the Seven Years War?), Parmentier existed on a prison diet of very little but potatoes – and remained healthy. After the war, the trained pharmacist took a greater interest in nutrition, with a particular focus on the foodstuff that had kept him alive. He was also something of an early PR man, organising assorted publicity stunts to promote his beloved vegetable. One of these, an all-potato dinner for members of France's high society, is said to have included Thomas Jefferson, who, at that time, was America's commissioner in Paris. When Jefferson became president, the story has it that he served fried potatoes, in the French style, to his guests. And that could well have been the birth of French fries in the USA. Even if it isn't strictly verifiable, it's definitely worth a bluff.

Noodles are no longer just noodles. If you don't know your *udon* from your *soba*, or your *idiyappam* from your *kway teow*, then serious kudos can be lost in a matter of seconds.

A GLOBAL MENU

An introduction to international cuisine is another big ask. After all, you could fill entire libraries with books on French food alone. However, your goal here is not to gain a comprehensive knowledge. It's about looking for ways to make your knowledge *look* comprehensive.

You don't need to know everything, but you do need to have at hand a few salient points on a variety of cuisines and, particularly, some obscure dishes. People love to drop the names of obscure dishes into food conversations, and the use of foreign words is seen as an opportunity to look knowledgeable and highly experienced. Food worshippers are frequently the same personality type as those people who will correct you when you say something like, 'Oh, I'm off to Paris tomorrow.' 'Oh,' they'll say, correcting your pronunciation, 'I adore "Paree".' (Sadly, you are not allowed to set about them with a cast-iron frying pan.) But there is still some value in dropping foreign words into food-related conversations.

For example, noodles are no longer just noodles. They never were, of course, but now if you don't know your *udon* from your *soba*, or your *idiyappam* from your *kway teow*, then serious kudos can be lost in a matter of seconds. You could actually write *The Bluffer's Guide to Noodles* and still not cover everything in enough detail, so learning the difference between a few and just avoiding noodle-based conversations is recommended unless you're feeling confident. For the record, those just mentioned are thick Japanese noodles, Japanese buckwheat noodles, Indian rice noodles and flat, thick rice noodles from Singapore, respectively.

There is also considerable value in knowing the details of the uniquely challenging dishes of a particular culture. Bravado eating is the culinary equivalent of going native, a badge of honour that gives an air of superiority over those who wouldn't attempt such food. A small knowledge of such things is therefore useful, as it will enable you to maintain a conversation without ever having to eat Italian cheese that's riddled with maggots, French sausages that have a whiff of ordure about them, or bits of a Japanese fish that, if incorrectly prepared, could kill you.

Here, then, are just a small selection of the most popular world cuisines, dishes and products – and unusual delicacies – to improve your bluffing abilities.

JAPANESE

Yakitori While often used to describe all snacks grilled on skewers, technically *yakitori* means 'grilled chicken' or 'grilled bird', depending on your source. It can encompass any part of that bird, though, such as the *shiro* (small intestines), *nankotsu* (cartilage) or *sunagimo* (gizzard).

Kushiyaki 'Grilled on a stick', and the word that you can use for anything non-chicken that's been stuck on a stick and, well, grilled. *Yaki*, as you may have deduced by now, means 'grilled'.

Unagi Freshwater eel and, more specifically, a freshwater eel that's been grilled, then steamed and grilled again, and then basted in a slightly sweet sauce.

SUSHI

The word that covers all dishes involving cooked, vinegared rice and, usually, seafood. But you can get much more specific than that. For example...

Nigiri/nigirizushi The one that you generally know: the oblong of sushi rice covered with a slice of fish.

Maki/makizushi The cylindrical sushi roll, with the seaweed – sorry, the *nori* – on the outside and cut into several pieces.

Futomaki Translates as 'fat rolls', which is not what you'll get when eating this healthily. As the name suggests, it's *maki*, only bigger.

Temaki The cone-shaped one. It translates as 'hand roll'.

Uramaki *Maki* has the seaweed on the outside of the rice. *Uramaki* has the *nori* on the inside. Perhaps unsurprisingly, *uramaki* translates as 'inside out'.

Sashimi Slices of raw fish without rice.

Shirako Cod sperm. Sushi made with the sperm sac is a

delicacy in Japan.

Fugu Feeling lucky? Try the pufferfish. Rather charmingly, the literal translation of *fugu* is, apparently, 'river pig'. It's a lovely name for something that, incorrectly prepared, will kill you in a particularly nasty manner. Its organs – particularly the liver – contain tetrodotoxin, a poison that will paralyse but leave you conscious before you eventually shuffle off due to asphyxiation. Chefs have to be specially trained before preparing *fugu* for human consumption. The resulting *sashimi*, served in very fine slivers, is oddly bland and strangely crunchy. You may wish to speculate that it's all about the adrenaline rush.

CHINESE

It should be stressed that most of the next few dishes have a huge variety of spellings. That's a result of the various translations and, where possible, the most pronounceable are used – hence *har gow* here instead of, for example, *xiā jiǎo.*

Har gow Shrimp dumplings. There should be at least seven and, ideally, more than 10 pleats on the dumpling; this is a measure of the dim sum chef's abilities.

Char siu You don't have barbecued meat in a Chinese – specifically Cantonese – restaurant. You have *char siu*. Or, very possibly, *chasu, cha siu* or *cha shao* depending on who's written the menu. The translation is 'fork roast'.

Hirata For many years, Chinese steamed buns have been

known as Chinese steamed buns. Now, though, they're *hirata*. To be fair, they probably always have been in China, but now only the ignorant would call them anything but *hirata*.

Shumai Those basket-shaped pork dumplings shall no longer be known as basket-shaped pork dumplings. They will be known as *shumai*. Or, indeed, *shu mai, shao mai* or assorted other variations. Again, the most famous version – pork, minced shrimp, and mushroom – is Cantonese in origin.

In some parts of the world, fresh protein comes in the form of *gou rou:* dog meat.

Gou rou In terms of psychological challenges, many have – and will continue – to declare that horse is just another meat. However, in some parts of the world, fresh protein comes in the form of *gou rou:* dog meat.

FRENCH

Where does the bluffer start? The 'Glossary' (*see* page 113) is as good a place as any, not least because it's mostly in French. And it's a good idea to remember a few names of famous French chefs to drop – Parmentier, Carême, Escoffier, etc. Although it might currently be *de rigueur* to say that French food isn't what it was, try telling that to the French. And, oddly enough, it's still the language of *haute cuisine.*

SPANISH

Spanish food is often celebrated as some of the purest, most straightforward and simply delicious anywhere in the world. In claiming this, you have the added bluffing value of distancing yourself from the type of holidaymaker who has colonised vast swathes of the Spanish coast and introduced the All-day Full English Breakfast. Instead, you will be demonstrating that you are the type of food connoisseur who's spent many idle weekends wandering Barcelona's La Rambla and famous food market La Boqueria, consuming your body weight in *tapas* (snacks) and *raciones* (portions).

That distinction is important. A *tapa* is a tiny serving, typically offered alongside a drink. A *racion* is a larger portion. For the record, while we're on the subject – and because this is precisely the sort of distinction you need to be making – a *pintxo* is served on a stick. (You may also come across the term *montadito* – meaning it's served on bread.)

You also need to understand the difference between the grades of the ham known as *pata negra*, for, as you may state with confidence (and because it's almost universally agreed upon), Spanish ham is the best in the world. If the subject comes up, the bluffer should simply say 'Ahhh... Serrano... estupendo...' (but try not to sound like a voiceover for an advert). In the context of Spanish ham, the bluffing potential gets even better; for example, wherever you see the term *jamón ibérico* you must remember to refer to the ham as *pata negra*, as that is the more accurate global term for the three main varieties available. All must be made from the meat of the Ibérico pig, and a pig can only be declared as such if its parentage is at least 75% pure Ibérico. *Pata negra* translates as 'black hoof' or 'black foot', a distinguishing mark of this breed. The finest grade of ham in the country (and therefore, probably, the world), *jamón ibérico de bellota* comes from free-range pigs that roam oak forests (known as *dehesas*) and feed on acorns. As a little extra, a producer called Joselito is regarded as producing the best *pata negra* in Spain. Remember that name, and repeat it whenever you are offered *jamón*.

ITALIAN

How many pasta shapes are there? Good question. In fact, you could argue that there are only a handful of shapes – long and thin, tubes, twisty, round, seed-shaped, shell-shaped, assorted others – but in many different sizes. And, perhaps not surprisingly, many of the different sizes have different names. A knowledge of a few of these offers some subtle bluffing opportunities.

For example, *orzo* is rice-shaped. *Risi* is the same, but is slightly smaller than *orzo*. After that, there's *puntine* which is a smaller size of *risi*. Similarly, you may know *farfalle* pasta, as it's the one in the bow-tie shape, but did you know that there's a smaller one called *farfalline* and that another variation – bow-tie shaped but with more rounded edges – is known as both *tripolini* and *farfalle?*

Another joy of Italian food is how the 'traditional and authentic' recipe for just about any dish or sauce will be prepared in a completely different 'traditional and authentic' way in the neighbouring village or region. Both are right, meaning both are also wrong. There are regions of the country where feuds probably still simmer over the type of cheese that should be used in *ravioli.*

POSH NOSH

According to the dictionary, 'gastronomy' is the practice or art of choosing, cooking and eating good food. Bluffers should be prepared to debate about whether gastronomy is an art. Your position is that these days it's closer to a religion.

Gourmet cuisine is ubiquitous. Once upon a time, it remained behind the doors of a prohibitively expensive fine-dining establishment and you could ignore it if you chose. Now you can't avoid it. Pubs have become gastropubs or 'pub dining rooms' and are being snapped up by Michelin-starred chefs. Greasy-spoon cafés are increasingly able to explain the provenance of everything in the pan, on the counter or in a sandwich. Tiny local restaurants are playing with 'molecular gastronomy' or cooking their locally sourced, seasonal, artisan pigeon livers in a water bath for 11 days at 17 degrees.

Where do you begin making sense of it all? In truth, you probably don't need to. This end of the eating world is somewhat bizarre and full of contradictions. It's frequently at the mercy of assorted fads and fashions, yet also riddled with convention. It's arguably where the cutting edge of cuisine takes place, but it frequently celebrates the traditional. It's also where the Venn diagram for playfulness and stupidity intersects.

Take, for example, the great Ferran Adrià – often described as one of the leading proponents of molecular gastronomy (although he refutes the tag) – which, as you will know, is an interest in the physical and chemical transformations of ingredients that occur while cooking. Adrià is the man who helped take the legendary Catalonian restaurant elBulli from a one-time minigolf-course bar serving drinks and sandwiches to being named the world's best restaurant four years in a row. One of Adrià's trademark dishes was olive-flavoured liquid chemically altered (via a process called 'spherification') into an olive shape. It thus looked like an olive and tasted like an olive. Other places achieve the same result by just giving you an olive. Cutting edge, gimmick or fad?

Happily, such contradictions make for great bluffing, and pointing out these contradictions a) makes you look informed and b) means you don't have to actually answer the question. Simply raise an eyebrow.

Interestingly, as more and more people are attempting to bring better and better food to the masses (who seem to be slowly responding), and as the cutting-edge techniques from the likes of Adrià and Blumenthal filter down even to pub menus, the bluffer should be aware that there has been something of a growing resistance to 'high-end dining'.

Among a certain class of food worshipper, there is a trend

currently in vogue to maintain that gastronomy is overhyped. Not for them are elaborate meals, precise cooking techniques and beautifully arranged plates of food; now is the time to celebrate simple dining and street food – a return to basics.

The great irony is that, at the same time that he or she purports to renounce fine dining and multi-course tasting menus, the food worshipper will very likely have a checklist of the great dining establishments around the world that they are eager to visit (or will claim to have visited already). And while they claim that they're more at home in the food stalls of a Moroccan *souk* or on the street-food trail around Austin, Texas, they'll tell you all about their favourite restaurant in the world, which you'll discover is all crisp tablecloths, tasting menus and *amuse-bouches**, and has at least one, probably two, Michelin stars.

Hypocrisy? Yes. But just go with it and nod sagely, while simultaneously ensuring that you have a basic grasp of the Michelin star system. However much food worshippers waffle on about the 'purity' of simply cooked and freshly sourced food, no bluffer worth his or her salt is ever going to denounce the ultimate guide to gourmet cuisine.

RUBBER STARS

You may wonder why a name associated with tyres is also associated with fine dining around the world. The guide started in 1900 as an *aide-memoire* to French motorists,

* *See* 'Glossary', page 113.

listing useful things such as petrol station locations and where to find good things to eat. Over the years, the guide evolved into probably the most famous restaurant guide in the world.

The main rankings that people focus on are the Michelin stars, awarded to a very select few places, on a scale of one to three. How select? Consider the number of restaurants across the globe. What are we looking at? Hundreds of thousands? More than a million? In 2012, only just over 100 establishments worldwide had the coveted three stars.

The scale breaks down as follows:

One star – a very good restaurant in its category.
Two stars – excellent cooking and worth a detour.
Three stars – exceptional cuisine and worth a special journey.

A favourite accusation levelled against the *Michelin Guide* is that it only rewards a very particular kind of place – generally somewhere with subtle decor, uniformed waiting staff and traditional table service that follows the old French ideals of what constitutes fine dining. To be fair to Michelin – and to show your own great understanding of international eating – there has been a shift in recent years to accommodate more modern styles of dining. In the UK, for example, there are pubs with Michelin stars – The Harwood Arms in London's Fulham, The Royal Oak in Maidenhead – and even one – The Hand & Flowers in Marlow – with two stars; and there's a good spread of other star ratings across a variety of restaurants and cuisines, from Japanese to Indian, via Italian and Chinese.

There are other criticisms levelled at the *Michelin Guide* which bluffers should know about. For example, there are many regions that the guides simply don't cover in Africa, the Indian subcontinent, South America and most of Eastern Europe. In addition, US Michelin stars tend only to be awarded in a few key cities – New York, San Francisco, Chicago and Las Vegas among them.

At least one chef has allegedly committed suicide as a result of being downgraded by Michelin.

Another complaint surrounds the pressure it puts chefs under to maintain standards and to conform to a mystery set of guidelines. To date, as far as the general public is aware, at least one chef has allegedly committed suicide amid fears of downgrading. In 2003, the day before the new *Michelin Guide* was published, Bernard Loiseau is rumoured to have shot himself after reports suggested that his restaurant, La Côte d'Or, was going to lose one of its three stars. It may have been a catalyst, but Loiseau was also reportedly suffering depression and debt problems before this point. The story is told rather well in Rudolph Chelminski's book *The Perfectionist*, a fact you may wish to drop into Michelin-related conversations when

Loiseau's name inevitably comes up. You may also wish to comment, with an appropriate sense of gravitas, that the book is a fine analysis of the pressure in restaurants in general. Whether you've read it or not.

So, to recap, you can affect to both loathe and love the *Michelin Guide*. Openly use it to help create your wish list of international restaurant experiences, at the same time as brazenly criticising it and picking holes in every aspect of its philosophy. This is essentially how food worshipping works.

As a reaction to the *Michelin Guide*, many people will cite the World's 50 Best Restaurants Awards, organised by *Restaurant Magazine*, as having a closer grip on what it is that diners actually want and which is far more global in its scope. The latter point is well made (so do make it again at any opportunity).

Rather than trail through the *Michelin Guide* or the World's 50 Best Restaurants for a list of places that you should say are on your wish list, simply have a few key names up your sleeve; those listed below are as good a place to start as any. Remember: it's not just about the name and reputation; it's about food being right, and having a sense of time and place. And with that in mind, it's a good idea to add some great food destinations – just to demonstrate the breadth of your knowledge of these things.

NOMA, COPENHAGEN

Noma is famous for taking local and seasonal to its Danish extremes. Unless it can be found naturally in the country, the restaurant doesn't serve it, hence no olive oil or exotic ingredients. You can, however, have ants, bulrushes, live shrimps and flowers.

What to say Depends on the current stance. At the moment, this is still a culinary altar at which you must worship. Give it another year, however, and it could be passé. Either way, Noma is still at the forefront of a major revolution in food. Hence, it's on your list.

HAWKER CENTRES, SINGAPORE

The 'street-food capital' of the world, which is a strange reputation, as Singapore doesn't really have any street food. Instead, the food stalls – some 15,000 of them in a place about the size of the Isle of Wight – are spread among (currently) 107 government-licensed, off-street 'hawker centres' (the inspiration behind our own soulless 'food courts' in shopping malls). Some suggest that this means the place has lost a certain energy.

What to say In food terms, Singapore is a hybrid of cultures and culinary influences, with Chinese, Malaysian, Arabic and Indian food combining to all sorts of interesting effects.

EL CELLER DE CAN ROCA, SPAIN

Located in Girona, El Celler de Can Roca is, at the time of going to press, the new number one in the World's 50

Best Restaurants list. It is run by three brothers – Joan, Josep and Jordi Roca – whose mother had a restaurant in a working-class suburb of the city. Joan is the *sous-vide*-loving head chef. Josep is head sommelier and runs front of house. Jordi is the pastry chef.

What to say The cutting-edge cooking remains close to its Catalan origins, but since winning the Best Restaurant award, the waiting list for a table is currently a year and

> Peruvian restaurants are springing up in London faster than you can skin a guinea pig.

there is a backlog of 3,000 requests. Suggest that if you can't wait, the best bet is to go to Rocambolesc, the restaurant's ice cream shop, so at least you can say you've 'eaten' there.

MAINE, USA

The East Coast of the USA is famous for its seafood – in cafés, restaurants, diners, trucks and little shacks. Lobster rolls are the classic dish, and you could find around 18 different versions in the same stretch of coastline. Deep-fried belly clams, however, are the best local 'secret'.

What to say Arguably 'the seafood capital of the world'. Shake your head in mild frustration and speculate as to why

Maine's residents have such a fantastic choice of brilliantly cooked, fantastically fresh fish at just about every eating establishment, while the UK ships the great majority of its catch to Europe.

CENTRAL, PERU

Lima is the unexpected location for Central, a new entry which made number 50 on the 2013 World's 50 Best Restaurants list. Young chef Virgilio Martinez has worked in all sorts of kitchens – learning things about Japanese, Vietnamese, French and Italian cooking which all feature in his food – alongside the Brazilian influence of his partner and co-chef Pía León.

What to say Peru is *the* new place to eat. Peruvian restaurants are springing up in London faster than you can skin a guinea pig (but probably not a good idea to mention guinea pigs). Having touched on the importance of South America as a food provider to the world, it's perhaps thus fitting that Peru is starting to get its place in the culinary limelight.

THE OLD BISCUIT MILL, SOUTH AFRICA

You want edgy? Come to Cape Town. While its reputation may owe more to violence and crime than good food, every Saturday, in the appropriate setting of The Old Biscuit Mill, some 100 local speciality traders sell fantastic food and produce. South African food in general has a growing reputation – great seafood, excellent grilled meat and brilliant wines.

What to say Try bunny chow, a hollowed-out loaf filled with curry, in its place of origin before it inevitably becomes a British street-food craze in the very near future.

SUSHI AT TSUKIJI MARKET, TOKYO

There is no shortage of options for sushi at Tsukiji, the enormous fish market in Tokyo. The fish is so fresh, a decent vet with a needle and thread could probably get it swimming again.

What to say If you're going to set a benchmark for Japanese food, then this is the place. But don't forget to express your moral concerns about the fishing industry;

The fish is so fresh, a decent vet with a needle and thread could probably get it swimming again.

there are, you can speculate, few better illustrations of how we're overfishing than several thousand square metres of downtown Tokyo overspilling with freshly caught fish every day of the week. And that's just one city.

CORNWALL, UK

The UK has to feature somewhere in your wish list, and Cornwall is doing lots of good things. It also has something of a microclimate, and a great sense of history and community. Cornwall is also far enough away from other parts of the UK for you to make up all sorts of things about its food scene and will rarely be caught out. Also, while we may make comments about TV chef Rick Stein's takeover of Padstow – 'Padstein', as some will have it – his influence has helped boost a rather impressive local food movement.

What to say Given the above, anything you like, really... but stress how wonderful it is to know that somewhere in the UK it's still possible to buy fresh fish and see not only the water where the fish was swimming that morning, but also the boat that caught it. Words like 'proper' are an effective punctuation here.

‘I’m a little over burgers. I’m more interested in trying that new Franco-Scottish twist on the sausage roll I read about on Twitter.’

FASHIONABLE FOOD FADS

Fads never die out, of course. They simply change. But at the moment, fads seem to be fundamental to food's status in popular culture. That means that, while you might have a keen understanding of food trends at the time of writing, you will have to keep an eye out and your ear to the ground for the inevitable shifts and changes of heart.

Bear in mind that fads have a habit of coming around again – and again – so you can always pass off an old fad you know about as The Next Big Thing. If questioned, just say that it's 'a new take'; and/or that it started somewhere in the sticks (in which case attribute your knowledge of it to any form of social media); and/or combine it with another fad you remember and call it 'fusion'; and/or keep it straight and just declare it 'post-ironic reinvention'.

BURGERS

In the past few years everyone has started talking about burgers. You might be sick of them and could have blinked and missed the latest developments. Here's an example:

It's a twist on the chip-shop burger; it's artisan-produced, dry-aged beef smothered in Marmite, kimchi and strawberry jam and deep fried in a tempura batter made with microbrewed American IPA, served on this AMAZING Latvian brioche roll.

You can either nod and make appreciative noises *or* bluff hard in return, either on the same theme or with your own classic dish. Nodding is safe, but bluffing is a lot more fun. For example:

I hadn't heard about the latest chip-shop burger. But have you heard about the 'reverse' burger? It's a new take from a bakery stall at a little farmers' market in Truro. It's a sesame brioche bun wrapped in minced beef, sandwiched between two slices of tomato, served between big slices of pickled cucumbers and lettuce leaves.

Or

Chip-shop burger? Fascinating. I'm a little over burgers, though. I'm more interested in trying that new Franco-Scottish twist on the sausage roll I read about on Twitter. It's from an old family bakery in Aberdeen, apparently. The grandson of the founder married a girl he met in Paris, and it's a twist on his family's scotch pie recipe served in a deep-fried sourdough croissant.

Nobody will question you. Indeed, someone will probably claim to have already tried it.

So, what do you need to be aware of in order to stand your ground? Here are a few fads, trends and other things of which you need to be aware, as well as some suggested opinions you might like to have on each.

BLOGGING

Ever heard the joke about opinions being like sphinctery bits of the anatomy? That everyone's got one? Thanks to technology, not only does everyone have an opinion, but now they can air that opinion to the entire world. Or, more specifically, the entire world with Internet access. Or, even more specifically, the very small percentage of the population with Internet access who give a monkey's about such things.

Online diaries became rather easy to set up and maintain. These were known as 'web logs' which quickly evolved into 'blogs'. There are millions of them, but one of the loudest and busiest sectors is food blogging.

Many people (particularly journalists and other media types) dismiss them for their terrible writing, unqualified opinions and the aforementioned bottom-themed reference. Others love the bloggers: some are good writers, typically able to respond to new openings and trends quicker than print titles and more likely to find interesting local spots. The truth, as you'll no doubt want to mention, is that, like 'professional' journalists, some bloggers are great and funny and enthusiastic and informative, but many are opinionated oafs who don't know their artisan from their elbow. The debate will rage on, but you should remain above it, a voice of confident reason seeing the good in all sectors.

INSTAGRAM

For convenience's sake, all amateur food photography can be included under this heading. Thanks to Instagram, it now appears that food cannot exist or be tasted unless one has provided proof by taking a series of photos of each beautifully assembled plate or, more likely, each messy, cheese-oozing slab of comfort eating.

Instagram is an app that allows you to take photos, give them a filter – to boost colours, make them look like 1970s Polaroids – blur bits of them (because depth of field is suddenly bizarrely trendy), and then share them with your followers, people on Twitter and so on.

A huge number of photos on Instagram are of plates of food, funky street-food stalls and well-marbled pieces of beef. If it's edible, someone will have taken a picture of it. The rest of Instagram is self-portraits – or 'selfies' as the kids call them. Most of these appear to have been taken by the popular singer known as Rihanna.

GOURMET BURGERS

As mentioned, one of the more popular sectors of the food service industry is the one that specialises in cheese-oozing comfort eating. This is not a recent thing: millions of people around the world are inordinately fond of comfort eating, in whatever shape it comes – wrapped in bread or pastry, or atop mounds of mashed or fried potatoes. However, in recent years, many favourite, mostly American, fast-food pleasures have been 'revolutionised' and taken significantly upmarket.

For the most part, this is a fad that shows no sign of

stopping. In a few short years fast food has gone from the high street to the high end of the street. Many highly rated restaurants offer their version of the burger. These can range from simply good beef to the ludicrously expensive Japanese Wagyu beef, to the deep-frozen horseburger with the whip marks still visible.

Even normal, non-food-worshipping folk are now enjoying quality 'gourmet' burgers on a regular basis in what has become something of an unstoppable burger craze. Bluffers should take the view that it is just meat in a bun, after all, and the fact that some chefs are making them with better meat, cooking them juicily rare, topping them with properly melted cheese and serving them in a well-sourced bun with dill pickle is not really cause for the level of worship accorded the dish. Line cooks in US diners have been doing this more than adequately for years.

One position for the bluffer to take is to deem yourself an expert in an utterly random burger-related field and then rate all subsequent burgers on an arbitrary scale. In order to give this credence, you need to give it a name (such as a US city or state). Nod sagely as you take your first bite. Chew contemplatively. Stare into the middle distance for a second or two. Declare your opinion firmly, for example: 'It's good… It's not quite a Philly burger, but it's good.' Nobody will ask what you mean but, if they do, just pull the bun apart, show the burger and fillings in cross section, shrug your shoulders and say 'See what I mean? It's just not quite Philly, is it?' You can always make vague references to texture, the use of pickles and/or the melting point of the cheese if they push you further.

Things to point out in general gourmet-burger-related conversations include the quality of the meat, the contrasting crunch of the pickles and the type of bun used. The general consensus is that the beef should be freshly ground and seasoned after cooking (salting in advance will dry it out). Any cheese should be the worst, processed, plasticky kind (and laughed off as a guilty pleasure), the bread probably brioche but anything in proportion that holds its shape while being soaked in beefy juices is deemed acceptable. And there should be a little textural contrast; white onion, dill pickles, etc. are all acceptable.

GOURMET HOT DOGS

Texture comes into play when analysing the hot dog, too. As many restaurants have added a gourmet burger to their repertoire, huge numbers are following suit with hot dogs. A recent survey – Horizons' Menurama survey to be precise – found that gourmet hot dogs were on 85% more menus in 2013 than they were in 2012.

It is, you may wish to point out again, simply a sausage in a bun. Things you're looking for here are, again, the quality of that bun, the quality of the toppings and, particularly, the texture of the sausage. The key to the hot dog, you can state with authority, is the 'snap'. That's the little bit of resistance as you bite into the sausage, and many say that each bite should have the same effect.

As for 'authenticity', people are rather freer in terms of what's allowed in the hot-dog world than they are with burgers. Anything goes – absolutely anything from chilli to peanut butter and all points in between, potentially at the same time.

GOURMET FRIED CHICKEN

A few light years beyond the KFC version, upmarket fried chicken is now spreading like wildfire. As you can imagine, the quality of the chicken is the selling point, together with the cooking process – brined, soaked in buttermilk, left alone, and so on – and the quality of the coating. *Panko* – a Japanese breadcrumb – is often held up as the perfect outer layer. What you're after, though, is texture: a crunch and tender meat. And if it's good-quality, free-range chicken, you can enjoy it because your conscience is untroubled.

WHAT'S NEXT?

You can expect to see gourmet burgers in myriad forms on all sorts of menus for years to come, alongside more posh fried chicken and more smartened-up hot dogs. What's next remains to be seen. Burritos have already swept across the country, with dedicated stores (and US chains) nationwide. The hash – essentially leftover meat and potatoes fried and served with an egg – has already started making appearances on various modern menus (and it's been on older menus for years). Maybe, you can say, it's time for something else.

BRITISH FAST-FOOD FAVOURITES

Fish and chips and the pasty

Traditional fish and chips made the transition to gourmet menus some time ago, at mark-ups of up to 500% of the shop price. Perhaps the traditional pasty is next. It is, after all, a thing of beauty. If your knowledge of burgers, hot dogs, chicken and other variations on the meat-in-a-bun theme is limited (or you're just bored with the constant worship of things from over the Atlantic at the expense of our own food culture), then use this to your advantage. Allow your eyes to moisten soulfully, recall that moment you first bit into the rich pastry, and declare it ripe for national revival.

Scotch eggs

There is some evidence that one such UK revival is gaining momentum for an unexpected old favourite. The scotch egg has become a stalwart of pub and restaurant menus in recent years. The spelling is correct, by the way: it has nothing to do with Scotland. To 'scotch' is an old term meaning to cover with meat. The story goes that a regular and important customer of Fortnum & Mason needed a handheld snack that they could eat in their carriage. The result was something similar to a haggis-wrapped hard-boiled egg. That subsequently evolved into mystery bits of minced reclaimed pork slapped around battery farming's finest, coated in luminous orange breadcrumbs, plastic-wrapped and sold in petrol stations.

Recently, that's changed. Scotch eggs are being made with care and quality ingredients, and served warm, so that the yolk is still runny. Some restaurants have attempted to 'improve' on the recipe – venison, black pudding, all sorts of other things – but there's a purity that you should celebrate in the more common pork version. After all, you may wish to point out, bacon and eggs is one of the more successful marriages of ingredients in British food history. As is ham, egg and chips. There's history between the pig and the chicken...

Kebabs

There is often speculation that the humble kebab is also ripe for a move onto gourmet menus. This typically comes from people who aren't Greek, Cypriot, Turkish or, indeed, any combination of the three. Many Greek, Cypriot and Turkish-run kebab shops build up their *shawarma/doner* (the familiar rotating vertical spit) each day from good-quality, marinated pieces of lamb or chicken. Not for them the mystery 'elephant's foot' of reconstituted, unidentified meat product.

The pleasures of fast food aren't hard to fathom. Fat tastes good; it's like God's cruellest joke. You can analyse it further; people respond to grease, sweetness and, particularly, texture, although they might not realise it. They will once you've enlightened them. The salad, the pickles, the breadcrumbed crust are important. Use words like 'mouthfeel' and 'bite', analyse each mouthful, pull things apart to investigate them closer. Even if you don't know what you're looking for, it looks like you do.

STREET-FOOD FADS

The rise in street-food culture is an important one to acknowledge. People who've run successful street-food ventures are moving into their own restaurants, while people who have learned their trade in restaurants are frequently taking their food to the streets. So as the classic handheld, late-night snacks have found themselves poshed up on restaurant menus, a wider range of international dishes has simultaneously taken to the streets.

If there's one thing you must love more than food from a truck or a car boot, then it's food in strange places.

It is, you will argue, a great moment in food democracy – a chance for individuals with a bit of culinary talent to start their own business without the need for massive investment. It's also early days, so expect to see this spread further from London and the big cities to the rest of the UK. The breadth of things being served – from Indian snacks to highly creative BBQ offal dishes and Mexican food by way of Korea – is also the sort of opportunity that has advanced bluffers hearing a chorus of celestial angels as the conversation moves this way. The people you're talking to will be hunting the streets of major metropolises to find the latest, most authentic, most cutting-edge food offering out there. Feel free, then, to mention the Ethiopian/Chilean fusion stall you found the other day doing *injera* wraps with sea bass *ceviche* and spicy, coffee-infused lentil curry... The beauty of street-food stalls is that they move around, spring up without warning and just as quickly shut down. That's obviously what happened to the one you will claim to have found when your friends can't track it down. The same thing will probably happen to that Italian/Ghanaian stall with the *jollof arancini* you'll discover next week, swiftly followed by the Spanish/Malaysian place with the *rendang tortilla*.

POP-UPS

If there's one thing you must love more than food from a truck or a car boot, then it's food in strange places – particularly when it's not a permanent fixture. The pop-up craze comes in various forms but is exactly what it sounds like – food businesses 'popping up' in the most unlikely of settings for a limited period of time. This could be a day, a single day a week – tea-and-cake pop-ups in antiques and vintage fashion shops, for example – or for a week, or four. (Rather inevitably, you may wish to comment, the 'big boys' are attempting to cash in on the hipness of the term, hence Jamie Oliver's press people declared his Diner project a pop-up. A three-year pop-up, in fact. That's not a pop-up, of course: that's a short-term lease.)

In some cases, it's a wonderful opportunity to test a new food idea without massive overheads. The fact that it will probably attract the Instagramming, blogging types is a bonus. In other cases, it's so archly trendy, it reeks of desperation as people throw themselves at the bandwagon – and often miss it altogether.

RAMEN BARS

To re-emphasise the point, noodles are no longer just noodles. They're *udon*, *soba* and so on. They're also fantastically trendy.

One of the big fads in London recently – so expect it across the rest of the UK in the next year or two – has been the rise of *ramen* bars, partly because 'ramen' sounds so much better and cooler than 'noodle soup' but mostly because it's cheap, hearty and absurdly delicious. Feel free to describe it as a new generation's Pot Noodle.

LOCAL AND SEASONAL

In bits of the UK, the local and seasonal thing is somewhere between mantra and restaurant philosophy. The thing is, and what you need to point out with your impressive understanding of 'eating with the seasons', is that in most parts of the world (and, indeed, in many places in the UK), local and seasonal isn't a cliché to shout about; it's just what they've always done. Reminisce about those childhood picnics you possibly never had and the taste of the tomatoes you picked straight from the vine (or possibly didn't). When you've had food that fresh and seasonal, why would you want vegetables that have been flown from halfway around the world?

SMALL-PLATE DINING

And finally... The 'tapas' idea is wonderful in Spain but, over the last few years, has expanded to include every kind of restaurant. Lots of them now don't offer 'starters' or 'mains'; it's 'small' and 'large' plates. Many establishments have taken it even further and offer everything as small plates. This is an ingenious way to mix and match and try many different flavours and dishes – and an even more ingenious way for a restaurant to make you spend 50% more than you realised.

You can frequently tell when you're in such a place because your meal will be prefaced with a patronising comment such as: 'Have you eaten with us before? No? Then let me explain how our menu works...' This can be deeply annoying but don't succumb to the temptation to reply: 'Do I order food from it and do you then bring it? Yes? Then I don't need it explaining.'

The small plate thing will also result in a line about 'and chef will send dishes out from the kitchen when they're ready, not in any particular order.' Again, resist the urge to say: 'Is chef paying for my meal? He's not? Then he can send the dishes out in whatever order I want them,' and smile politely, even as they explain that you probably need five small plates to make a satisfying meal. Each. Relax. One day, small plates will be replaced by the highly revolutionary concept of starters and main courses.

It is almost your duty as a bluffer to take an alternative stance, to question the blanket acceptance that GMOs – genetically modified organisms – are the work of Beelzebub. You can silently agree, of course.

A MATTER OF MUTATION

One of the joys of bluffing is being contrary. More precisely, one of the joys of bluffing is being contrary and having the key points at your fingertips in order to back up your contrariness.

Genetically modified food is a great case in point. The standard accepted position – unless you're an employee of GM giant Monsanto – is that genetically modified food is pure evil. It is almost your duty as a bluffer to take an alternative stance, to question the blanket acceptance that GMOs – genetically modified organisms – are the work of Beelzebub. You can silently agree, of course. Indeed, in your new role as an expert food lover, words like 'artisan producer', 'organic' and 'local smallholding' should pepper your conversation at the best of times. However, an acknowledgement of the potential need for GM foods and the ability to see both sides of the argument makes you appear well-informed and impressively analytical.

Statistics, as we regularly state, are your friend. A few choice facts, backed up with a percentage or two, can suggest a level of knowledge and understanding that far outstrips the reality. The GM debate has many statistics of note. A particularly good one to support the argument for modified crops – or to simply declare as you lament the state of the British food industry – is the '14 August' theory.

A KEY DATE TO NOTE

The rise of GM foods is related to the ever-increasing population of the planet. The demand on natural resources increases day by day. In 1991, according to the National Farmers' Union, the UK produced the equivalent of 75% of the food the nation consumed. In 2013, however, that figure had fallen to just 62%. That means, were the UK forced to be self-sufficient, the nation's supplies would run out on – you guessed it – 14 August.

UNDERSTANDING GMOs

This, you can argue, is evidence that we need GM crops. Or further farm investment. One thing you will notice in any conversation about GMOs is that, beyond the 'work-of-Satan' standpoint and the need to feed a growing population, a large number of people know very little about them. This is thus typical of modern life, and a glorious gift to the bluffer in you.

For example, what exactly is a GMO? In much the same way you can now point out the flaws in the authenticity question, the GMO definition is open to debate. It is very possible to argue that just about every crop in history has been genetically modified. The concept of root stock is relevant here; all fruit trees, for example, are grown from cultivars that have been spliced to roots of a different species. The cultivar has been cultivated to produce fruit. The roots are chosen to suit the soil in which it's been planted. You can state with reasonable conviction that this, surely, is a genetic modification. You also need cross-pollination for such things to survive and produce fruit. Does cross-pollination count? It's a question worth asking – mostly because if you ask it, you don't have to answer it. At that point, you can get away with an admission that, no, you don't know the answer, but it's an interesting question.

To some extent, in order to produce more fruit or larger yields, or to reduce pest problems, mankind has been genetically modifying/tweaking plants for years. Only a few plants worldwide – broccoli, is said to be one – can be traced back to one single plant.

THE FISH TOMATO

Generally speaking, however, such splicing and cross-fertilisation is not considered genetic modification. The 'bad' GM – depending on what stance you're taking – is when scientists splice genes from one species to another. For example, some tomatoes that struggled in colder climates have been genetically modified with the gene that protects a fish called the winter flounder against cold-water temperatures in the depths of the Atlantic. The result? A tomato that doesn't suffer in the frost.

The implication is that all such genetic engineering is the territory of the mad scientist and thus dangerous and evil. However, before you grab a flaming torch and pitchfork and attack the labs at Monsanto and their assorted rivals, there's a chance to question the health issues. In the case of the 'fish tomato', both products involved are edible. Also, as you might like to remind people, it's not the best business policy in the world to kill your customers. It really doesn't do anything for repeat sales. Ostensibly, the 'fish tomato' is perfectly safe. By all means have the moral debate, and question whether there should be full disclosure on such products, but rest assured that they're safe to eat. You can back up this statement by pointing out – with a certain piety – that the likes of the American Medical Association, the European Union and the World Health Organization have tested GMOs thoroughly and declared them safe and healthy – although, of course, they would say that…

In some cases, GMOs may be healthier than alternative options. A fine example is the addition of a gene from a bacterium called *Bacillus thuringiensis* into potatoes. *Bacillus thuringiensis* is naturally occurring, safe to humans and toxic to the Colorado beetle, the pest that is known to destroy potato crops. The kneejerk reaction against GMOs saw the *Bacillus thuringiensis* gene research stopped and replaced with a conventional pesticide – later found out to be deadly to the Colorado beetle (hurrah) but also potentially harmful to the developing brains of mammals, like, well, human beings. Whoops.

Much of the fierce opposition is due to the name – genetically modified organism – and the fact that it smacks of Frankenstein-esque unnatural experimentation. The GM companies should really have gone with 'food tweaking' or something similarly cosy. A more concrete argument against GM, though, is that any such manipulation of the food chain is unnatural and wrong. While you might get different breeds of dogs mating, or donkeys and horses, or lions and tigers, on the rare chance that a winter flounder and a tomato would ever get frisky, there certainly wouldn't be any cold-proofed resulting offspring.

It's not the best business policy in the world to kill your customers. Ostensibly, the 'fish tomato' is perfectly safe.

A more reasonable reason to express concern is that GMO research is frequently funded by the likes of Monsanto and DuPont, the companies with the most to gain from GMO development.

So, you've got a few options in your GM bluffing stance. As the world's food supply fails to meet ever-increasing demands, something perhaps has to give. The same argument applies to the current prediction that insect protein will be The Next Big Thing; after all, insects are no uglier than fish and just as full of protein. And they're a popular foodstuff in Southeast Asia. (You might also have noticed that there's no shortage of them, unlike fish.)

LAB-GROWN MEAT

On the subject of fresh sources of meat, however, insect protein might not be the only answer. As you may have heard, in 2013 a lab-grown burger was cooked and eaten at a London news conference.

Although it's not essential bluffing knowledge, you never know when it might come in handy to know how to grow a burger. In this instance, a Dutch institute took stem cells from a cow, added nutrients and growth-promoting chemicals, and let the stem cells multiply. After three weeks, these had grown into a million stem cells forming small strips of muscle. These were then formed into pellets and frozen. And then, when there was enough to make a burger, they were defrosted and formed into a patty and cooked. The verdict from those who got to try it was 'close to meat', so you can insert your own fast-food joke here.

Why grow meat other than as livestock? See above. The world's population is growing at a rapid rate, a large percentage wants to eat meat, cows take up a lot of space we don't have and, even if the space were available, they produce a lot of methane which is a bad thing for the ozone layer. Hence non-flatulent, lab-grown beef is possibly the future. Although, to be fair, it probably won't work as a tag line. The fact that the burger cost US$330,000 was widely quoted but a tad misleading; the research cost US$330,000, the burger – and many subsequent bits of protein – very little.

So, what position to take as a bluffer? Again, asking the unanswerable question is a fine gambit. A sense of gravitas and a question on whether this means that lab-grown meat is vegetarian is thought-provoking and distracts from the more specific details and facts. Another question worth raising – and certainly easier to ask than answer – is whether GM foods and non-farting lab beef are solving world hunger or merely addressing the symptoms. Should that much protein be consumed by human beings? Would better distribution systems make it easier for farmers to grow food that hasn't got bits of fish in them? What happens if lab-grown meat grows a brain? It lives! Should the question be thrown back at you, the recommended response is to raise an eyebrow again. Who knows? The whole issue is open for discussion, isn't it? Wiser heads than yours will be spending many hours debating this one, right? There are two sides to the story. You can see the pros and the cons, and sometimes the fence is the most comfortable place to sit.

'If you start with good ingredients, then you don't need bows, whistles and Smarties on the top.'

Darina Allen, Ballymaloe Cookery School, Ireland

SHOPPING AROUND

Shopping, they say, is 80% of the battle when it comes to preparing good food. Actually, they don't say that at all. Sounds convincing, though. See how easy this is?

As the rules of eating and, particularly, the rules governing our attitude to food have changed, then so have the rules of shopping. A few years ago, food shopping went something like this: look in cupboards, look in fridge, compile list, visit supermarket, buy things on list, buy many things not on list, come home.

These days, food shopping goes something like this: look in cupboards, look in fridge, check organic vegetable box, check calendar for details of next organic vegetable box delivery, check calendar for details of next organic meat box delivery, check the recipe you tore out of that Sunday supplement to see just how much quinoa and how many pounds of Jerusalem artichokes you need, call organic vegetable box company, go to supermarket for basics, go to butcher, request birth certificate and family tree of the piece of beef that you're considering buying, pop to local market to discuss the week's cheese requirements with a producer of artisan washed rinds...

For the sake of punctuation it can be left there, but you get the point. The rules haven't just changed; they've packed an entirely new wardrobe, had plastic surgery and emigrated.

To be fair, shopping well is a useful skill. Yes, some of the food worshippers' shopping techniques have become a middle-class cliché (and the reason why children throw almighty strops in Islington delis, screaming 'But I wanted SUN-DRIED tomatoes!'), but if you start with good ingredients, you don't need to do anything to them to make them taste good. Darina Allen, who runs the acclaimed Ballymaloe Cookery School in Ireland, explained it thus: 'If you start with good ingredients, then you don't need bows, whistles and Smarties on the top.' That's a very useful 'simplicity-is-key' quote to drop into many food conversations.

You don't, of course, have to do all of the aforementioned. You can just go to the supermarket and pretend that you know what you're doing. But a knowledge of how to pick good ingredients is useful for the sake of your own taste buds and to enforce your claim as a highly knowledgeable food-worshipping type. It's also not just a case of spending the sort of sums on the weekly shopping that used to buy a week's holiday. Bargains score you brownie points in this world, ditto an address book of great local shops. Simply put, insider knowledge is cool.

SHOPPING CLEVER

Striking up a relationship with a local greengrocer can be a worthwhile experience, particularly if they'll sell you (or even give you) bags of bruised fruit that they can't shift. While there's a certain amount of kudos attached to having the perfect apple on display in your fruit bowl, there's potentially more if you can explain that your pie filling was a planet-saving, ecologically sound use of fruit otherwise destined for the bin. Similarly, stews made from scraps and cuttings from the butcher – or from discounted, near-to-sell-by-date packages from the supermarket – are at least as equally eco-credible as a cut of organic rib-eye that cost more than your first car. When it comes to that look of piety that adds so much quality to your bluffing, this would be a case in point. And, of course, you don't have to become best buds with your greengrocer and butcher; you can just pretend you have. 'Oh yes,' you can declare, as you serve a soup that you bought from Tesco on your way home last night, 'Harry always saves me the broken broccoli heads…'

Shopping tips, whether you employ them or not, sound good. A knowledge of seasonality will also make you look smart. For example, don't serve fresh asparagus in February; look carefully and they'll have Peru or China stamped all over them.

This modern frugality is a strange contrivance, but revel in it. It's superb bluffing material and improves your disposable income – a win-win in anyone's book.

HITTING THE BINS

A few key bits of advice also make you look extremely canny – for example, knowing when to hit the supermarkets for the reductions. These typically happen around an hour or two before closing. Waitrose, you might like to note, often has things like Poilâne sourdough bread in the discount bins which, by anyone's standards, is a great product (even at a tenner a loaf). It also freezes brilliantly. Your food-worshipping guests will be delighted if you serve them a slice of something artisan that you picked up at the farmers' market that morning, but equally delighted with a defrosted bit of bargain toast. 'Yes,' you can declare, 'would you believe I found a whole loaf of Poilâne for a pound the other day? I know, right? One can only assume that less well-informed shoppers don't have any idea just how good it is...'

Another fine fact to demonstrate your fully rounded knowledge is where exactly to find the bargains. Supermarkets have spent millions researching how you shop and, by now, are exquisitely engineered merchandising machines designed to make you spend, which is why the cheaper products are rarely at eye level (but you can bet the profitable ones are) and why impulse buys like sweets are placed near the tills. A little awareness of supermarket design allows you to offer some well-informed advice. For example, have you noticed how the store layout makes the majority of customers walk the same way around the shelves? As an experiment, try changing your usual path around your local supermarket and count how many times you're in the way and walking against traffic. Also, take a look at how often the same colour scheme used for discount signs is employed on regularly priced purchases, which leads punters to assume that they're getting a bargain even when they're not.

This is a bizarre world you're entering, but just go with it. The same people who want to know the parentage of the chicken they're eating will also get a buzz that you've bought – or at least claim to have bought – your basics at the German-owned global discount stores Lidl and Aldi. You might add, simply to further your air of in-depth retailing knowledge, that it is a myth that the two supermarket chains are owned by competing brothers who fell out. But if you feel the need to further fascinate your mesmerised audience, tell them that Aldi opens a new store in the UK approximately every week, and that one of Lidl's UK stores is built on the former Battle of Britain airfield in Hawkinge, Kent. This always gives rise to the spirited old argument about who actually won the Second World War.

SHELF LIFE

So, other key bits of wisdom to casually announce… A very quick way to establish your food credentials is to despair at people's inability to smell the difference between something that's genuinely off and something that's just past its best-before/use-by date. Some will argue that you *must* eat something by the use-by date because otherwise it might kill you, while going past the 'best before' is what gives you some wiggle room. Just bear in mind – and drop into conversation – that supermarkets are paranoid about being sued, so the dates printed are much shorter than they need to be. Besides, if milk is off, you'll know. You'll definitely know. And if it's really off, so will your neighbours.

Eggs are easy to spot as well, and there's a fine old-wives' method which you can employ to demonstrate your expertise. Drop the eggs into cold water. If they sink and stay at the bottom of the bowl, they're fine to use. If they float to the top, bin them. Eggs are pretty dense when fresh but the shell is porous and, as the egg ages, moisture escapes and air gets in. Floating eggs have thus been exposed to a lot of air and will have deteriorated.

The most effective opportunity to announce your shelf-life knowledge, however, is in the case of cheese. Some people will throw out cheddar because it's just gone past its best-before date. Shake your head sadly and explain that cheese is merely a milk storage system. In the case of cheddar, it's already 12 to 24 months old, so how on earth would another day make a difference?

Here are some other key things you should know about particular foodstuffs when shopping and, in due course, make sure other people know you know.

FISH

Some people are terrified of buying fish. Indeed, there is a strong argument that, unless you were present when it came out of the water, there is no knowing how fresh – or otherwise – it is. This is, clearly, not very practical.

What you should be looking for in terms of whole fish is shininess. The eyes should be bright, the fish itself should look clean and metallic, the gills should be a rich red; dull eyes, dull skin and dull gills are not good signs. Ironically, fish shouldn't smell fishy. It should be fresh-smelling – odour-free but for a hint of brine.

If you're looking at filleted fish, the flesh – and any skin – should be vibrant, as above. Again, you want a clean odour – nothing fishy. The prod test (*see* page 72) is a good one; anything that puts you in contact with the product looks like expertise.

Basically, the rule of thumb is that signs of recent life are a good thing – whether dead, whole fish, already in sections, or, in the case of lobsters and crabs and such, still moving around. In the case of the latter, if it's got a semblance of vitality, get the Thermidor sauce ready.

As for frozen fish, generally speaking, as a budding/bluffing food expert, it is a good bet. Frozen fish lose little moisture and are usually frozen very shortly after being caught.

AVOCADOS

One big food disagreement is over the definition of the perfectly ripe avocado. For the people aiming to eat one, the avocado should be soft, yielding to the touch without being mushy, a deep, uniform green, and free from bruising. For the people running the supermarkets, 'perfectly ripe' apparently means 'consistency of a cannonball'.

This discrepancy has, like your opinion of the Gypsy

Kings or whether you're watching season three of *The Killing*, become acceptable dinner-party conversation and a delightfully middle-class joke. By all means crack it, or laugh when someone else says it, but be prepared to spin this opportunity into smart advice on just how to get the perfect avocado. That advice is to buy your avocados rock hard and let them ripen at home.

For the people running the supermarkets, 'perfectly ripe' apparently means 'consistency of a cannonball'.

Transporting a slightly ripe avocado, you see, will bruise it terribly. Rock-like ones will get to the fruit basket unscathed and, in a few days' time, should be utterly perfect. Also, to ensure that they're perfectly green within rather than streaky and brown, brush away the dry stem on the avocado. If what's underneath is green, there's an extremely good chance that the fruit is uniformly green within. If you reveal a brown looking patch of flesh, the chances are that there's nothing you can do to make that avocado better. Even if you've never bought an avocado in your life and never will, the least you can do is improve somebody else's shopping.

MEAT

Obviously your friendly local butcher – the one with whom you're on first-name terms – will be carefully selecting all your joints and chops for you. But a little knowledge of meat shopping is nonetheless useful. Again, first and foremost, start with something good (a tip you'll no doubt drop into conversation on a regular basis now), and you don't need to ponce it up with a jus, a twist of this or, indeed, Smarties on the top.

Many elements are simply a case of taste. Others will, of course, tell you that steak *has* to be dry aged for at least 35 days otherwise it's just not worth bothering. This, as you should by now have spotted, is utter nonsense. If it's a bad piece of steak from a poor cow, no amount of ageing – dry, wet or otherwise – is going to improve the flavour. Also, and much more importantly when holding your own in such debates, it's all a matter of taste.

In dry ageing, cuts of beef are stored at near-freezing temperatures for several days and the moisture in the beef evaporates, which concentrates the beef's flavour. In addition, over time, the beef's natural enzymes help break down the connective tissue in the meat, which helps tenderise it.

In wet ageing, the beef is vacuum-sealed to retain moisture. The meat can't 'breathe' and is effectively marinated in the fluids that would otherwise evaporate. The result is a faster ageing process, but one that's generally regarded as inferior. Unless you prefer the taste which, frankly, millions of Americans seem to.

Dry ageing for 28, 35 and 45 days is common in certain butchers and upmarket steak restaurants. The results depend on the cut, the cattle and what you prefer. At the risk of over-simplifying, at around 28 days there's a certain gaminess. At around 35 days, that flavour is slightly subdued. At 45 days and over, the meat starts to develop something of a sweetness. But all can be good and all have their fans. There is no right answer, as you should clearly explain to people.

Arguably more important is the level of marbling. This is a word that *must* be added to your food vocabulary and refers to the amount of fat running through the piece of meat. Fat tastes good. For beef – but also lamb and pork – a piece of meat that contains nice, relatively even flecks of white fat through the muscle is what you're after. Essentially, while cooking, the fat melts and bastes the meat from within. The swirls of white resemble the patterns in marble, hence the name.

Other things to look for are smell, texture and colour. The first one of those three is easy; if it smells off, don't buy it. This can be tricky if it's film-wrapped in a polystyrene tray, but you can always take it back if in doubt. As for texture, squeezing is good. Gentle prodding is also good and not only suggests a level of expertise but genuinely helps identify a decent cut. A good piece of meat should give a little and spring back into shape when you squeeze it or press it gently. If it doesn't, move on. As for colour, avoid green – 'whatever Dr Seuss may have said in *Green Eggs and Ham*,' you may wish to add – but look for dark red beef and lamb, and pink (not grey) chicken and pork.

One way to suggest a knowledgeable attitude to meat is to suggest 'cowpooling'. In much the same way that you can purchase barrels of whisky while they're ageing somewhere in a distillery, you can cowpool your animal protein – i.e., purchase an entire cow, pig or sheep with some friends and receive shares of the meat when it's killed. Inviting people to cowpool with you demonstrates your concern for farming standards, your love of quality meat and your knowledge that such arrangements exist. Side of beef, anyone?

A food that makes you lose weight as you eat it – how wonderful would that be? On the downside, if such a thing existed, it would probably taste like celery.

FOOD MYTH CONCEPTIONS

There are all sorts of myths about food and, as far as you are concerned, that is a very good thing. The half-known, frequently misunderstood 'fact' is often the bluffer's golden ticket – an invitation to enlighten and inform.

There are numerous commonly misheld beliefs. The perception that Belgian chocolate is superior to all others is a good one, as is the contention that 70% chocolate is the minimum one should settle for; anything less just isn't good enough.* Or the 'fact' that oysters are an aphrodisiac, that salads are the healthy option, that you burn more calories eating celery than you consume... The list goes on.

A scant knowledge of the truth behind these commonly held beliefs is still significantly more than most people possess. Here, you'll find the rundown on some of the most frequently repeated, providing you with the ammunition you need to confirm them or gently point out why they're wrong.

* See *The Bluffer's Guide to Chocolate.*

BELGIAN AND 70% CHOCOLATE ARE BEST

Many recipes call for Belgian chocolate, or 70% chocolate, as if this is an indication of quality.

The Belgian thing is pure marketing spin. There are, undoubtedly, some fine Belgian chocolate makers but there are also some terrible ones. The key points to make, though, are that Belgium neither grows cacao trees nor has a minimum standard for the chocolate produced within its borders.

You are, of course, aware that the 70% notion refers to cocoa solids. As you may wish to point out, that could be 70% frankly terrible cocoa solids. And what about the other 30%? Nobody ever questions what's in that, do they? The answer is sugar and cocoa butter, and perhaps milk powder and/or vanilla, but it could be anything: animal, vegetable or mineral.

OYSTERS ARE AN APHRODISIAC

Ah, the old chestnut. The evidence is typically the historically apocryphal – Casanova breakfasting on 50 oysters a day – or the fact that these shellfish are packed with zinc, a mineral known to have a positive effect on sperm production and, potentially, libido. A recent(ish) study, however, found that bivalve molluscs – the group of shellfish to which oysters belong – are rich in two amino acids, D-aspartic acid (D-Asp) and N-methyl-D-aspartate (NMDA) (worth remembering). These acids, when injected into rats, resulted in increased testosterone production in males. That doesn't mean, as you may wish to point out, that they'll have the same effect on humans. So there's evidence to suggest the theory is true – and evidence that, actually, maybe it's not? Regardless, there's wiggle room which, coupled with an understanding of both sides of the debate, leads to fine bluffing opportunities.

DECAFFEINATED COFFEE HAS NO CAFFEINE

Frankly, that's not the case. Minimum international standards are that decaffeinated coffee must be 97% caffeine-free; EU standards are stricter, at 99.9%. So, there's still probably some caffeine in there, albeit in minuscule traces.

What you may wish to consider, however, is the process involved in removing this level of caffeine from coffee. Caffeine is extracted with the use of solvents, which include ethyl acetate, methylene chloride (dichloromethane, or DCM) or supercritical CO_2. Mmm, tasty. Particularly when you consider that dichloromethane is also used in paint stripper. That's a compelling point to raise with the requisite tone of gravitas, as you perhaps suggest that, instead of decaffeinated coffee, people should try another, less chemically altered drink instead. But maybe not green tea...

GREEN TEA CONTAINS NO CAFFEINE

Green tea is often suggested or selected as a low-caffeine option. Hold it right there. As you will now state with absolute confidence – because it's true – green tea has just as much caffeine as any other tea. Because it all comes from the same plant, *Camellia sinensis*, be it black, white or green tea. Green tea is less processed, that's for sure, but it has exactly the same level of caffeine as any other tea.

YOU BURN MORE CALORIES EATING CELERY THAN IT CONTAINS

A food that makes you lose weight as you eat it – how wonderful would that be? On the downside, if such a thing existed, it would probably taste like celery. Sadly, however, this myth is incorrect.

It is, undoubtedly, a very low-calorie food. A stick of celery, being mostly water, contains around six calories. An average woman, for example, sitting down and eating, is said to burn approximately 30 calories an hour. So yes, if you just ate a single stick of celery and took an hour to do it, you'd be some 24 calories ahead of the game. But, as you'll no doubt point out with considerable authority, what are the chances of that?

FAT-FREE FOODS AND SALADS ARE ALWAYS GOOD FOR YOU

These are such widely held beliefs that the marketing material speaks directly to those who assume it's true. Everything from chocolate to salad dressings, from beer to bread to breakfast cereal, comes in varieties that promise they're 'fat-free', 'low-fat' or 'now with reduced fat'. These imply that they're healthy products and will help you lose weight. However, fat tastes good and is frequently what helps flavour food products. Removing or reducing it changes the flavour, and manufacturers frequently add sugar and chemicals to rectify this. This is labelling that deserves to be questioned and a fact that needs to be pointed out.

As for salads, fresh leaves and vegetables are, of course, good for digestion, general health, vitamin content and so on. Cover them in a dressing made with oil, bits of bacon, grated cheese, etc., and you're looking at something that's potentially as calorific as the kind of main course you're

> Green tea is less processed, that's for sure, but it has exactly the same level of caffeine as any other tea.

trying to avoid. At one point, McDonald's offered a Caesar salad which proved to have a higher calorific value than a standard burger (425 calories and 21.4g of fat, compared with 253 calories and 7.7g of fat).

ABERDEEN ANGUS IS AN INDICATOR OF QUALITY

You will often see Aberdeen Angus on menus and at the supermarket. It's there as a shorthand for good, pure, Scottish meat. That is, as you've no doubt guessed, some distance from the truth. It's probably also some distance from Aberdeen.

Aberdeen Angus is a breed. It's not a brand. It can thus be farmed anywhere – not just Scotland. It has also, you are advised to point out, been crossbred to grow larger and thus give more meat. There is plenty of good Aberdeen Angus beef, but the name alone is no guarantee of quality. Meat quality comes down to how the cow has been fed, tended, butchered and how the meat has subsequently been aged.

The same applies to the acclaimed Bronze turkey, which gives you a lovely Christmas bluffing opening; the Bronze is a breed of turkey, not a brand name.

SCIENCE IN A SAUCEPAN

Statistics, as previously mentioned, are the bluffer's friend. A percentage dropped into conversation at the appropriate time lends considerable strength to your argument. Science plays a similar role. Most of us generally accept certain things about food without necessarily understanding them. An understanding of the subject, therefore – however small – can elevate what you say from humble opinion to unquestioned expertise.

Perhaps the best source of such things is the American food writer Harold McGee's book *On Food And Cooking*, published in 2004. This is a great read, endlessly fascinating and with more backup than you could ever possibly need. However, here are a few choice facts that will make you look like you know your onions.

A MATTER OF TASTE

The first question that people generally ask about food – aside from the damned authenticity debate – relates to taste and flavour. The joy of that is that taste and flavour, while connected, are different things. Taste refers directly to the taste of the food. Flavour relates to the personal combination of what we taste and smell.

As you may know – and certainly will in a few seconds – it has long been held that there are four tastes: sweet, sour, salty and bitter. This is the combination that provides the basis of most cuisine and, when you analyse things that taste good, you realise that it's the balance of these four points that are important.

Restaurants add monosodium glutamate (MSG) to their food because, frankly, it makes it taste better.

It is now generally accepted that there is a fifth taste: umami. This sort of translates as 'savoury', and is what gives certain foods that underlying depth and lip-smacking quality. It makes the roof of the mouth fizz or spark a little and it can be found in all sorts of things, from ripe tomatoes, mature cheese like parmesan and many meats, to things like soy sauce and Marmite, which are effectively pure umami. It's actually glutamate, a type of amino acid, that prompts this reaction. Hence many restaurants – famously the Chinese, but others, too – add monosodium glutamate (MSG) to their food because, frankly, it makes it taste better.

It is possible to pick all sorts of holes in this theory of

taste. Ayurvedic wisdom – and there's a word to make you sound knowledgeable – suggests that there are in fact six tastes, ignoring umami and adding in astringent (that sort of dry, mouth-puckering reaction you might get to tannins in tea or red wine) and pungent (the effect of things like chilli and mustard). Some scientists argue that there are seven, and that umami is too important to overlook. Some argue that there's yet another (a fifth, sixth, seventh or eighth depending on how you look at it) which is fat, as the mouth reacts in a different way to fatty substances. Some argue that chilli and mustard are different levels of pungency and thus perhaps need separate categories. Such contradictory ideas are bluffing heaven.

While this is an interesting debate, perhaps the most thought-provoking talking point is the difference between taste and flavour.

OLFACTORY SETTINGS

Flavour is a hedonic sense which refers to the fact that it pertains to pleasure. In this case, it's the pleasure derived from the combination of taste and the olfactory, because 'olfactory' sounds more authoritative and knowledgeable than 'smell'.

Scientists estimate that the majority of what we know as flavour comes from the nose. Indeed, it could be as much as 85%. If you want to demonstrate this to people, ask them to sip a glass of wine or eat a piece of strong cheese while pinching their nose shut. Take smell out of the equation and the flavour is diminished. The same logic applies when you have a cold. Your nose is blocked, you can't smell as efficiently, and thus food seems less appealing. It also applies when food is served at the 'wrong' temperature. Contrast freshly cooked bacon, straight from the pan, with a piece that has gone cold.

KNEADING THE DOUGH

Food and science are a marvellous combination because we take so much of it for granted. Take kneading bread, for example. (Resist the temptation to tell the one about making the bread because the baker kneaded the dough.) Why knead it? The simple answer is to distribute the yeast evenly throughout the bread. It's the yeast, as every budding cook knows, that makes bread rise. Kneading helps the bread rise evenly. It also helps break down the gluten.

Gluten is what you get when you mix water and protein (which, in bread's case, is present in the flour). Scientifically speaking, it's both elastic and plastic. That means it will change its shape under pressure, but tends to return to its original form when you stop. Kneading means that you compress and stretch the gluten, forcing and unfolding the molecules into a more orderly pattern. This makes the dough more stable, and makes it rise more evenly because the dough can now expand and incorporate the carbon dioxide the yeast is producing. Without that particular molecular structure, the carbon dioxide would just escape. When you think about it – and point it out to others – this simplest of recipes is an utterly perfect combination of ingredients and process.

BAKE OR ROAST?

You then bake it, of course, by putting it in the oven. Which is interesting, because when you do that to meat, you're roasting it, of course. So what's the difference? There isn't one. It's just become the convention. Technically both are a hot, dry cooking method; it's the air in the oven that cooks the food you've placed there. Some will argue – and you can argue it, too – that roasting is at a higher temperature – but, basically, it's all the same. If people insist on continuing the debate, simply point out what oven-cooked fish is called on a menu. Do you ever see 'roasted fish'? No. It's 'baked fish'. For some reason, convention has it that we roast meat and vegetables, and bake cakes, bread and fish.

THE SEARING TRUTH

On the subject of meat, how often do you hear someone say that you should brown or sear meat in a pan to seal in the juices? It happens a lot, and you can understand the logic: searing forms a crust and therefore the juices within will find it harder to escape. By keeping them in, you thus create a deliciously moist interior. The juices are sealed shut inside. Result.

It is, sadly, nonsense. The crust that's formed is not a waterproof seal. The purpose of searing is to add flavour. That's all. It's not a case of the browning process preventing juices and therefore flavour from escaping; the browning process actually creates flavour. It is also generally accepted that it makes the meat look better.

The reason for this is called the Maillard reaction, named

after Louis Camille Maillard, a French chemist who, if he hadn't been famous for this discovery, should have been famous for his glorious moustache.

You'll hear the browning process called caramelising, which is reasonably accurate. The application of heat causes a chemical reaction between an amino acid and sugar. The meat goes brown and basically tastes better.

If you're of a scientific bent, this is your opportunity to shine. Officially, the Maillard reaction is a form of non-enzymatic browning, where the reactive carbonyl group of the sugar reacts with the nucleophilic amino group of the amino acid, and forms a complex mixture of poorly characterised molecules responsible for a range of odours and flavours. Got it?

Browning doesn't just create a more attractive colour and a simple flavour profile, though. The Maillard reaction creates hundreds of flavour compounds. These then break down into yet more flavour compounds. It's all very clever, and explains why there's a greater depth of flavour – do throw in the 'umami' thing again here – in seared meat. There's another great example of the Maillard reaction, where the final, browned version of a foodstuff tastes significantly different from its unbrowned form. It's called 'toast'.

Physical reactions to certain foodstuffs are a very useful thing to comment on, suggesting a knowledge of food science that has considerable bluffing value. One of the most common is the reason onions make us cry. The simple answer? It's sulphuric acid.

Onions contain a volatile substance. It's not seriously

volatile, of course; you can't shake up an onion and disperse a crowd. But it is enough to make you weep while you're chopping. This 'lachrymator' – an agent for irritating the eyes otherwise known as tear gas – is released when you peel and cut an onion.

Peeling and/or cutting breaks cells in the onion, which allows their respective contents to mix. The reaction between some of these is what creates the tear-gas effect. Ready for the science bit? Amino acid sulfoxides form sulfenic acid, which breaks down certain enzymes to form a sulphur compound gas which reacts with the water in your tears and forms sulphuric acid. This makes the eyes sting and, in defence, they produce tears. This compound is seen off by cooking, although it's the same thing that makes raw onions taste as strong and hot as they sometimes can.

People still like to consult techniques and recipes actually written on paper, and preferably in a book. A butter-and-gravy-stained iPad is somewhat less desirable.

COOKING THE BOOKS

Sales of celebrity cookery books in the UK rose by 250% in 2012. It's a remarkable figure and one that almost sounds too unlikely for bluffers to pass off successfully. If that's the case, and you lack the confidence to persuade people that it's true, try these two facts on for size: The Hairy Bikers' diet book knocked EL James's *Fifty Shades of Grey* off the top of the bestsellers list; and Jamie Oliver's total book sales (as of 2012) totalled some £126 million, making him the second most successful UK author behind *Harry Potter* creator JK Rowling.

For some reason, even in light of just how many recipes are now available online, cookery book sales are bucking the general downward trend in physical book sales. The reason for this is unclear, but you can speculate that cookery and food are so deeply personal that people still like to consult techniques and recipes actually written on paper, and preferably in a book. A butter-and-gravy-stained iPad is somewhat less desirable.

If the eyes are the windows to the soul, as the old adage goes, then the bookshelf is the window to the palate.

Actually, it's not really, but there could be something in it. Many people claim that they can tell much about a person's personality by glancing at their bookshelves. Many also attempt to make themselves look smarter and more erudite, with unread Booker Prize winners on the shelves or with some other carefully chosen titles strewn artfully around the house.

So what are the books to have on general display? And which are you likely to actually use? Here's a guide to an instantly impressive food bookshelf, together with a selection of titles that you might actually use.

FOR THE BOOKSHELF

MODERNIST CUISINE

Talk about an instant bookshelf; *Modernist Cuisine* (published in 2011) is six volumes and 2,438 pages of incredible food science, analysis, recipes and photography, created by former Microsoft chief technology officer Nathan Myhrvold, Chris Young, who helped set up the experimental kitchen at The Fat Duck, and acclaimed chef Maxime Bilet. It's a beautiful, creative and complex look at flavours and textures, with detailed explanations (and cutaway pots) of cooking techniques from *sous vide* (a form of 'vacuum' cooking popular with the French) to barbecue. Recipes from the first five volumes have been compiled into the sixth with handy wipe-clean pages. With an RRP of £395, it represents maximum bluffing value. Get it, lovingly stain it and make those pages look well-thumbed.

The original *Modernist Cuisine* has spawned two further volumes: *Modernist Cuisine at Home* (2012), which does exactly what it says on the cover (and perhaps acknowledges that the earlier version wasn't the most accessible); and *The Photography of Modernist Cuisine*, which is a beautiful collection of jaw-dropping photography on a massive scale.

LAROUSSE GASTRONOMIQUE

The grandaddy of all modern cookery books? Very probably. It's certainly more up to date than Mrs Beeton's entry into the market. Fans – i.e., you – will declare it 'an unparalleled resource', 'essential to understanding the history of modern food and cooking techniques' and 'full of ideas on how to cook everything.' Detractors – again, you, if circumstances demand – will point out that, yes, the information is comprehensive, but the recipes don't work, it's only any good if you like French food, it's terribly outdated and, with the best will in the world, it's more the sort of food encyclopaedia you'd dip into rather than actually use for cooking.

While the French name suggests that this Larousse chap must have been something of a cookery god in 1938, Larousse was actually the publishing company. It may thus be easier for you to undermine the book's influence, should the situation require, as being, essentially, the equivalent of the *Reader's Digest Compendium of Cooking*. It was actually written by the splendidly monikered Prosper Montagné (1865–1948), a French chef with an impressive CV, an even more impressive knowledge of French cuisine and history, and a methodical approach, as the book covers every French region and just about every ingredient you could think of.

It is, whether you're a fan or not, as detailed a work on a particular cuisine as you'll ever find. Chef Anthony Bourdain agrees, calling it 'the bible of cooking' and 'the all-time argument ender.' As he says: 'Early in my cooking career, I wielded my *Larousse* like a weapon and it never let me down.' Paraphrase these comments at will. The book deserves its (non-sauce-splattered) place on the shelf.

THE FAT DUCK COOKBOOK

Less a coffee-table book and more a book that could serve as a coffee table, Heston Blumenthal's comprehensive look at his first restaurant, its history and the dishes that made it famous is, undoubtedly, fascinating. It's also wrist-threateningly heavy and, in many cases, you'd need a bigger kitchen to be able to open it. That's partly, you can explain, because you'll need a *sous vide* machine, a dehydrator, a vacuum pump and a nitrogen bottle in order to tackle some of the recipes.

There are some 50 signature recipes from the bespectacled, self-taught, so-called molecular gastronomist, including salmon poached with liquorice, snail porridge, and bacon and egg ice cream. Many are infamous, and most are notoriously hard to prepare without access to Heston's kitchen or a Bond villain's lair – and not that much easier, even if you do have all the gear.

However, it is a beautiful book and, as you can point out to anyone who'll listen, it's not just about following recipes to the absolute letter, is it? You use the book for inspiration, to show what can be done with imagination and wit and a grasp of flavours. And actually, it's not always about the completed dish, it's the journey, and there are elements

> Most recipes are notoriously hard to prepare without access to Heston's kitchen or a Bond villain's lair.

of certain dishes that are easily prepared and excellent. It must be said, though, that £40 or so is rather a lot of money to get a single French toast recipe.

FÄVIKEN

You could, of course, opt for the Noma book (*Noma: Time and Place in Nordic Cuisine*). As previously discussed, the rise of Scandinavian cuisine is too important to ignore in your new role as a food worshipper of repute. However, as more and more people are aware of Noma's approach, it's time to look further afield for inspiration.

Step forward, then, Magnus Nilsson of Fäviken in Sweden (the restaurant recently made it into the world's top 50) and his book which is not so much about the recipes as it is about the philosophy. The lustrously bearded Nilsson not only serves food that has been farmed, hunted or found within the immediate vicinity of the restaurant, he only uses ancient preservation methods and, on the basis that the old farmers of the region didn't have access to *sous vide* machines and liquid nitrogen, only cooks using the most straightforward methods – and for only 12 people a night.

The 'recipes' (vinegar matured in a burnt-out spruce tree, anyone?) generally involve ingredients you won't find this side of the Baltic – unless, perhaps, you have a local shop specialising in Finnish bitter milk caps. That offers you two choices. You can claim to have attempted a dish with ingredients you/your friend/a colleague/your mum brought back from Sweden. Or you can again acknowledge that this one is less about the specific details of the recipes and more about the inspiration and the purity of the ideas.

FOR THE KITCHEN WORKTOP

LEITHS COOKERY BIBLE

If it's good enough for graduates of Leiths… If you only take one book into the kitchen, there's a very good argument that it should be *Leiths Cookery Bible.*

As well as forming the basis of the renowned Leiths School of Food and Wine diploma, like *Larousse*, the book is a great go-to for whatever you're trying to cook. It's not what you'd call cutting edge, though – *Larousse* doesn't mention *sous vide* because even the update is old; *Leiths* doesn't mention it because, well, it's too damned funky.

As well as plenty of stains serving as bookmarks, the opening 100 pages must be genuinely well-thumbed, as they contain a ready reckoner of all the cookery information you will ever likely need, such as menu planning, conversion tables, freezer advice, wine, equipment and quantity calculations. Recipes also give all measurements in Imperial and metric, and all temperatures in Fahrenheit as well as Celsius. It's a deeply practical book. Don't expect pictures, but do expect great information and a brilliant foundation in decent home cooking. It's also the sort of book that chefs recommend rather than members of the public, and therefore provides subtle backup to your claims of food-based expertise. Insist that this one's hard to beat.

DELIA'S COMPLETE COOKERY COURSE

When it comes to a book you'll actually use, this dependable old favourite has few rivals. There are clear explanations of ingredients and basic techniques, simple instructions and good tips aplenty, plus conversion tables and lists of useful implements and utensils. Best of all, you will probably find copies in charity shops, as people less in the know than you have replaced their tatty old 1983 edition with something trendy and pointless. If you buy a new edition, we'd recommend placing it by the hob while you fry something in oil, leaving it open at a cake recipe while you enthusiastically beat an egg, and using a gravy-covered thumb to turn the pages of the 'Meat: Roasting and Pot Roasting' chapter.

ROAST CHICKEN AND OTHER STORIES

First published in 1994, Simon Hopkinson's *Roast Chicken and Other Stories* picked up good reviews, a couple of awards and very few sales. Always something of a chef's chef, Hopkinson had run his own places, opened Bibendum for Terence Conran, and left that to take up writing for a living. Hence the book, which first looked like it was going to disappear without trace.

And then suddenly in 2005, a panel of cookery writers, chefs and other foodie luminaries voted it the most useful cookery book of all time. As a result, there was a week where it outsold *Harry Potter.* There is absolutely no truth in the rumour that the panel might have had shares in it.

It is a fine cookbook – one that's more inventive than the previous two mentioned but with enough basics to give a decent grounding. The book is arranged alphabetically by ingredients: it runs Anchovy to Veal, with anything from two to seven recipes per ingredient. It's not comprehensive, as you will cheerfully report, but everything works and there are charming introductions to each dish that you may wish to read before you cover everything in gravy.

MADHUR JAFFREY'S ULTIMATE CURRY BIBLE

There are many choices of decent ethnic cookery books you should have to hand, but one of the best regarded – and easiest to follow – is *Madhur Jaffrey's Ultimate Curry Bible.* As you will acknowledge, Jaffrey has written many books before and many since, but as an overview of curries from India, Singapore, Malaysia, Thailand, Japan, Britain and even the USA to name just some of them, this is as good as it gets. It serves as an interesting outline of the spread of curries around the world – should you need to drop more food history into your conversation – but, best of all, it gives you a very good grounding in the use of different spices, a useful bit of knowledge that you can employ on many occasions. Mention that Jaffrey is not only a famous actress in her home country of India but is also said to be the bestselling Indian cookery writer of all time.

The food industry moves so quickly that entire careers can start and finish in not much longer than it takes to read this sentence.

NAMES TO DROP

The world of food has always attracted personalities. From the likes of Parmentier to the cheeky 'pukka' one, to the sweary, crumple-faced Scottish one, to the unblinking zeal of the bespectacled one, to the voluptuous, finger-licking, buxom one, to the shoplifting Wozza one, this is a world of larger-than-life characters and – more importantly – opportunities for name-dropping.

The problem here is that the food obsessives you will be conversing with will, all too often, drop in the names of people in the industry. These could be historic names you are expected to know, current names you are expected to know and future names you are expected to know. The first two categories will not present a problem. The third category is harder. The food industry moves so quickly that entire careers can start and finish in not much longer than it takes to read this sentence.

You will be faced with statements along the lines of: 'Do you remember X? He was sous chef at Y, under Z. B was there around the same time. Well, he and A have joined forces and launched a pop-up French/Cuban, bank-themed supper club called C. It's similar to D in Brooklyn but these guys are doing it all organically and E is doing the drinks and everything's being served on handwoven, biodegradable, hessian plates that F's wife sourced from a collective opposite G's smallholding in Umbria.'

If you feel a knowledge deficiency chasm beginning to yawn in front of you, simply fall back on one of the following sentences which can be applied in around 95% of these conversations:

'X? Name's familiar. Didn't he work at Noma under Redzepi?'

'Y? Name's familiar. Didn't he work at elBulli under Adrià?'

Or, indeed, for maximum bluffing points:

'Z? Name's familiar. Didn't he work at Noma under Redzepi and elBulli under Adrià?'

As previously discussed, you could also take the disarming option of admitting you don't know who or what they're talking about. It's something of an anti-bluffing bluff, but it demonstrates a degree of confidence and frequently allows you to steer things back to your own areas of expertise in due course.

Here, then, are a few of the historic and current names you should: a) know and b) drop into conversation occasionally to demonstrate your depth of knowledge.

RENÉ REDZEPI

Redzepi is the Danish chef and co-owner of Noma, a two-Michelin-starred restaurant in Copenhagen. From 2010 to 2012, Noma was considered the Best Restaurant in the World in the World's 50 Best Restaurants Awards. That's why every young, up-and-coming chef wants to spend time there and, in many cases, already has.

Redzepi's calling card is 'new Nordic cuisine', using only ingredients that can be sourced in Scandinavia. Hence you won't find olive oil, tomatoes or *foie gras* on the menu, but you will find bulrushes, lichen and musk ox.

As well as training in Copenhagen – at Restaurant Pierre André and later Kong Hans Kælder – the biggest influence on Redzepi's culinary philosophy was elBulli and Ferran Adrià. After dining there in 1998, Redzepi worked in the kitchen in 1999. He also spent four months at The French Laundry in California.

In 2002, at the age of 25, Redzepi was offered a head chef role at what was to become Noma. That opened in 2004. The Michelin stars followed in 2008, the Best Restaurant award two years later.

What to drop into conversation The local ingredients thing, the number of chefs who have gone through the kitchen at Noma (all of them, apparently) and, should you like a quote, René's statement that: 'For me cooking is something that is completely transparent and without pretence, that is honest and generous and has something true and original to it.' Just like the molecular gastronomists, then.

FERRAN ADRIÀ

Ferran Adrià was the head chef at elBulli and is regarded as the father of the 'molecular gastronomy' movement. This is the cooking philosophy that plays with the senses and food science. Adrià is famous for doing things such as flavoured foams and said he wanted to 'provide unexpected contrasts of flavour, temperature and texture. Nothing is what it seems. The idea is to provoke, surprise and delight the diner.'

He began his career as a dishwasher in Barcelona and then in the admiral's kitchen while he did his military service in the Spanish navy. He joined elBulli as a line cook in 1984. Later that year, he and colleague Christian Lutaud took over the kitchen after the head chef left. It was supposed to be a stopgap measure but the duo were never replaced. Lutaud left in 1987, leaving Adrià to turn elBulli into the legendary restaurant it became.

In 1990, Adrià and a business partner bought elBulli. Shortly after, influenced by chefs Michel Bras and Pierre Gagnaire in Paris, Adrià developed his avant-garde approach to cuisine. The restaurant closed in July 2011 and is due to reopen in 2014 as a 'creative centre'.

elBulli was voted the Best Restaurant in the World in 2002, 2006, 2007, 2008 and 2009 – still a record. Bluffers should mention it at every available opportunity and say that they feel privileged to have eaten there in its heyday.

What to drop into conversation Adrià once said that innovation is not about being first. 'What is important is not to be the first but to conceptualise it.' To illustrate the point, he cites that Roman soldiers wore miniskirts but it took Mary Quant to make them an iconic fashion statement.

JEFFREY L STEINGARTEN

Steingarten is not a chef but a fantastic source of meticulously researched information and very entertaining writing. A former lawyer, he became *Vogue*'s food critic in 1989. It's not the most conventional career path, but the legal world's loss is the food world's gain. He is almost unique among food writers in not hiding his love of 'candy', once commenting that 'one of President Ronald Reagan's great achievements was putting a jar of jelly beans on his desk.'

There are two collections of his *Vogue* columns: *The Man Who Ate Everything* and *It Must Have Been Something I Ate*. In the words of *The New York Times Book Review*, these titles are both 'part cookbook, part travelogue, part medical and scientific treatise'. He probably knows more about food allergies than any person alive.

What to drop into conversation *The Man Who Ate Everything* features a particularly good essay on salt, finding that it's only harmful to around 8% of the world's population. This should be mentioned whenever someone does that annoying health-kick thing of declaring, 'Oh, we never salt our food now.' Consider it revenge for the tasteless gruel they've just made you eat.

HESTON BLUMENTHAL

Bespectacled genius, molecular gastronomy guru or mad scientist? In terms of chefdom, these are not necessarily mutually exclusive.

A former debt collector, Heston is a self-taught chef. The story goes that his first paid kitchen job was at his own restaurant, The Fat Duck, which he started in Bray in 1995. Before that, he'd spent a week's work experience with Raymond Blanc.

Dishes at the three-Michelin-starred Fat Duck and his other restaurants have included meat fruit (chicken-liver parfait covered in orange jelly so it looks like a mandarin orange) and a fish course called Sounds of the Sea where the diner wears headphones playing the sounds of gulls and crashing waves to enhance the experience. 'We eat with our eyes and our ears and our noses,' argues Heston, suggesting that his shirts are probably in a terrible state.

What to drop into conversation Heston is famous for his rather unusual ideas, taking the concept of molecular gastronomy into the realm of some rather eccentric, sensory experiences. However, he doesn't like the term, arguing that it makes the practice of cooking sound 'elitist'.

JAMES BEARD

You might often notice that an American chef has a Beard Award. This has nothing whatsoever to do with interesting facial hair but is a mark of distinction conferred by the award system set up by American chef and writer James Beard.

Beard was born in 1903 and claimed that his earliest food memory was from the Lewis and Clark Exposition of 1905, held to commemorate the first expedition to cross the USA to the Pacific Coast a century earlier. Apparently it was observing 'Triscuits' (a US brand-name cracker) being made that changed his life.

'Isn't that crazy? At two years old that memory was made. It intrigued the hell out of me', he later admitted. Triscuits, however, don't appear to have featured much in his culinary career, which he embarked on rather late.

A trained actor, Beard lived in Paris for a while and became a confirmed Francophile. Returning to the USA, and struggling to make a mark as an actor in the 1930s, Beard and a friend started a New York catering company called Hors d'Oeuvre. His first book, *Hors D'Oeuvre & Canapés,* sprang out of that time. By 1955, he was an established TV personality and food author, and had established the James Beard Cooking School.

What to drop into conversation The Beard philosophy was to create good food, honestly prepared with fresh American ingredients and to defend and promote the pleasure of real cooking against the rise of convenience foods. Julia Child (*see* below) called him 'The Dean of American Cuisine'.

MARIE-ANTOINE CARÊME

Carême was one of the first proponents of *grande cuisine*, the remarkably over-the-top style of cooking which originated in Paris in the early nineteenth century. During the French Revolution, he found work in a Parisian chophouse – which couldn't have been easy for a kitchen boy with a girl's name – before being apprenticed to a pâtissier and then eventually opening his own shop.

Carême is famous for *pièces montées* – enormous confectionery window displays often based on elaborate architecture, from the Pyramids to ancient temples. He is credited with the invention of, among other things, the *croquante* (a brittle treat made with almonds and honey) and the brioche-like *solilemmes* which came to be called Sally Lunns in the UK.

After creating pieces for French foreign minister Charles Maurice de Talleyrand and Napoleon, among other leading figures of the French establishment, Carême also started creating main courses. Napoleon funded the purchase of Château de Valençay, just outside Paris, as a diplomatic social club for Talleyrand, who set Carême a challenge: create an entire year's seasonal menu without any repetition. The chef passed the test and worked there until the fall of Napoleon, whereupon he went to London and became chef to the Prince Regent (later George IV), before returning to Paris where he was chef to famous banker James Mayer de Rothschild.

What to drop into conversation Carême is also credited with inventing the *toque*, the famous tall chef's hat. That's why, in any conversation about the great kitchens of the world, he really merits a mention.

MRS BEETON

Isabella Mary Beeton is the author of *Mrs Beeton's Book of Household Management*, published in England in 1861 and perhaps the most famous cookbook ever published. Her qualifications? Being the eldest sibling in an enormous

Victorian family of more than 20 children and being married to Samuel Orchart Beeton, a publisher who had launched *The Englishwoman's Domestic Magazine* – a groundbreaking periodical for middle-class women – for which his wife wrote cooking and household management columns. These were later collated and sold under a single volume: *The Book of Household Management* – a guide to running all aspects of a Victorian house, from managing the servants to childcare.

What to drop into conversation Mrs Beeton died at the age of 28, possibly as a result of having contracted syphilis from her husband (although that was never conclusively proven). You might add that she didn't actually create the recipes; they were generally from other writers like Eliza Acton, but the Beetons never claimed they were original.

ANTHONY BOURDAIN

Arguably the man who, thanks to two rather good books, took an overwhelming enthusiasm for food to the masses, Bourdain is an American chef, author and, more recently, TV personality, appearing on Channel 4's *The Taste*.

Kitchen Confidential was the book that made Bourdain's name among everyone besides New Yorkers, who had long recognised his Brasserie Les Halles restaurant as the place to go for proper, no-nonsense, meat-heavy French cooking.

The book charts Bourdain's love of food from a family holiday in France as a kid to his career in kitchens, but also gives a fantastic glimpse into what goes on behind the scenes in the industry and the types of personality it attracts. This 'on-the-edge' idea, and particularly the follow-up/TV tie-in *A Cook's Tour* (in which Bourdain attempts to find the best meal in the world), has given him a reputation as the go-to man who'll try anything.

What to drop into conversation *Kitchen Confidential* has been much imitated and probably never bettered. It's the book you return to any time you feel your enthusiasm for food worshipping dwindling. Bluffers can also do worse than quote Bourdain's observation that 'Your body is not a temple, it's an amusement park.'

ELIZABETH DAVID

The doyenne of British food writing, a merciless scourge of bad British cooking and as famous for her *froideur* as her *fricassées*, there's a great case to be made contending that Elizabeth David did more to kick-start the British food movement than anybody else. And having managed to avoid TV celebritydom, she is also relatively unknown to many people who claim to know about food – which makes her a perfect name to drop.

Her enthusiasm for Mediterranean cuisine – and contempt for substandard cooking – sparked great interest in the 1950s and 60s. For many Brits still suffering the privations of post-war rationing, she was the first to introduce ingredients such as pasta, aubergines, olive oil and peppers to their diet.

A self-taught cook, David started writing articles on Mediterranean cookery for *Harper's Bazaar* magazine and subsequently collated these into what became *A Book of*

Mediterranean Food. It was hugely successful and a sequel, *French Country Cooking,* was commissioned, followed by *Italian Food.* Unusually for the time, she spent months in the various countries, immersing herself in local culture and collecting recipes and ideas.

What to drop into conversation There's no shortage of material to choose from. As well as revolutionising food writing in the UK, David had an infamously complicated love life, and was refreshingly outspoken on all sorts of things, from the word 'crispy', to what she saw as low Michelin standards, to 'fussy garnish' and, particularly, garlic presses, refusing to stock the latter at the famous kitchen shop that she opened. The late writer Auberon Waugh (son of Evelyn) declared that if he had to name someone who'd brought the greatest improvement to English life in the twentieth century, 'my vote would go to Elizabeth David'.

JULIA CHILD

Fame – and a cooking career – came relatively late to American TV chef and author Julia Child. Born in 1912, it wasn't until 1948 that she started on the course – literally – that was to change her life. Her husband, Paul, was assigned to the US Information Service at the American Embassy in Paris, and Julia attended Le Cordon Bleu cooking school. With two other women, she started L'École de Trois Gourmandes and the three collaborated on a book adapting French cuisine for the mainstream USA.

Mastering the Art of French Cooking came out in 1961 and remained the bestselling cookbook for five years. The response was so great that she was given her own TV show, *The French Chef*. It was a huge success, was syndicated across the USA and made Child a star.

What to drop into conversation Obviously there's her influence, her no-nonsense approach and her larger-than-life persona – Child was 6' 2" which helped her stand out. Then

> 'I was 32 when I started cooking; up until then, I just ate.'
>
> *Julia Child*

there is her central presence in the book and film *Julie & Julia*, the story of how an aspiring cook spent a year cooking everything from Child's *French Cooking* book (Child was played by Meryl Streep). Her cooking came in for much criticism for its high fat content. It didn't appear to do her any harm: she died two days before her 92nd birthday.

GEORGES AUGUSTE ESCOFFIER

Before Julia Child, though, was Georges Auguste Escoffier, the French chef's French chef. He was probably the man most responsible for what has become modern French cuisine, simplifying and modernising Carême's more traditional, fussier style of cooking, and publishing *Le Guide Culinaire,* which is still used today for its recipes, techniques and Escoffier's approaches to kitchen management.

Escoffier first learned to cook at his uncle's restaurant, becoming an army chef. He opened his own restaurant in Cannes, then moved to Monte Carlo, where he ran the kitchen at the Grand Hotel before leaving for the Hotel National in Lucerne, which is where he met Swiss hotelier César Ritz. The two formed a partnership and in 1890 were approached to run the kitchen at a new London hotel called The Savoy.

What to drop into conversation His influence is still felt across the world, but perhaps his most lasting, and ironic, achievement was to move to The Ritz in Paris where he introduced the notion of a British afternoon tea. It was such a success that the idea then came to London.

There's no point in pretending that you know everything about food – nobody does (not even the most obsessive of food worshippers) – but if you've got this far and absorbed at least a modicum of the information and advice contained within these pages, then you will almost certainly understand more than 99% of the rest of the human race about why food plays such a central role in modern culture. You will also know which great chefs and food writers to be familiar with, what you need to say when discussing them, and how to get by in any conversation involving creative cuisine. What you now do with this information is up to you, but here's a suggestion: be confident about your newfound knowledge, see how far it takes you, but above all have fun using it. You are now a bona fide expert in the art of bluffing on a subject which has transcended the practicalities of human survival to become one of the greatest art forms of the twenty-first century. And if you believe that, then you are a bluffer *par excellence.*

GLOSSARY

There are many wonderful words in the world of food and it is essential to add several of the following to your vocabulary. There is a natural bias towards French and Italian words and expressions because, as you're about to discover, everything food-themed sounds better in French and Italian.

L'addition The French word for that gesture when you sign the air with your hand.

Affumicato Italian for 'smoked'; a deeply satisfying word, it suggests a deep understanding of the cooking process.

Aigre-doux 'Sweet and sour' in French; a fine bluffing word as it encapsulates two cuisines in three syllables.

Al dente It's not tough, it's just resistant enough; the perfect texture of pasta, but can be used to describe vegetables or just about anything with resistance to a bite.

À l'étouffée In English, 'stew' sounds like a dull mix of meat and vegetables. In French, it sounds inspired.

Amuse-bouche In French, literally 'mouth amuser'. A bite-sized hors d'oeuvre served at the chef's whim at the beginning of a meal, it is intended to demonstrate the chef's approach but, most importantly, serves to keep you happy while you're waiting for your first course to arrive.

Andouillette A sausage made of pig nether regions which smells of pig nether regions; a bravado eating classic, and still potentially a big practical joke by the French on British food worshippers.

À point Medium rare. In French terms, this means a steak that has been lightly heated with a match.

Ardente Not to be confused with al dente, this is a more obscure Italian word meaning hot and piquant.

Beignet Frankly, if you just called it a doughnut you couldn't charge as much.

Biscotti If you called it a biscuit, you couldn't charge as much; Italian for 'twice cooked', incidentally.

Bleu Further down the scale from *à point*, this is the same piece of steak without the match.

Bocconcini You'll see this used to describe little balls of fresh mozzarella. It translates as 'mouthful.'

Bouchée The French word for *bocconcini*: 'a tiny mouthful'.

Buongustaio 'Gourmet' is a well-known French term for one who appreciates the finer edible things in life. This is the less familiar Italian equivalent.

Brûlée Would you eat something advertised as 'burnt'? You would if it was in French.

Carpaccio Thin slices of raw/lightly cured meat, popular as a starter in Italian restaurants. The name should be spelled with a capital C because the dish is named after a painter who was particularly famous for his use of blood-red paint.

Casu marzu A traditional sheep's milk cheese from Sardinia. Don't be surprised if it wriggles as you attempt to eat it. It's flavoured with live maggots.

Chiffonnade Your disappointing meal had some frilly lettuce and vegetables as a garnish. Call it a *chiffonnade*, however, and it becomes something nigh Michelin-worthy.

Eau du robinet French for 'tap water'. Sounds better.

Fumé French for 'smoked'.

Granita Give people frozen, sugary icy wine or fruit juice and it sounds unappetising. Go Italian and give them a wine or a lemon *granita* and it's heavenly.

Julienne Slivers of vegetables which frequently come stacked in a Jenga-like pile. People go to catering college to learn how to do that. Nobody really knows why.

Latte While short for *caffè latte* in non-Italian-speaking parts of the world, ask for one in an Italian café and you'll get a glass of milk.

Marmite Yeast spread mined in Hades by orcs or woven

in heaven by angels, depending on your viewpoint. It's actually the French word for the little covered pot that appears on the label, hence it's a casserole.

Mornay Smother something in cheese sauce and it sounds like you're hiding something. Call it a *mornay*, though, and it immediately sounds more impressive.

Panna cotta An Italian dessert that, according to tradition, should move like a lady's chest bits when the plate is nudged. The translation is nothing rude, though; it simply means 'cooked cream'.

Ragù A meat sauce for pasta, but can be applied to any sauce involving ground or finely chopped bits of meat. You could slop some mince on someone's plate…or you could serve them an elegantly crafted *ragù*.

Salami As you know, an Italian sausage made of ground, cured meat that's been seasoned and shaped like a sausage. Serve more than one kind, though, and you have…

Salumi Which is the correct collective name for *salami* and similar cured meats.

Stufato Here's a beautiful and precise Italian term. *Stufato* is a stew; however, if the pieces of meat are smaller, then the stew is called a *spezzatino*.

Zeppole If a Scottish fish-and-chip shop offered you a fried pastry, you'd think they were having a laugh. In Italian, however, it sounds positively mouth-watering.

BLUFFING NOTES

Bluffing Notes

Bluffing Notes

Bluffing Notes

Bluffing Notes

Bluffing Notes

Bluffing Notes

Bluffing Notes

Bluffing Notes

Bluffing Notes

Bluffing Notes

NEW EDITIONS

Hold your own in any situation with these new and forthcoming Bluffer's Guides®

ACCOUNTANCY
BEER
BOND
CARS
CATS
CRICKET
CYCLING
DIY
DOGS
ENTERTAINING
ETIQUETTE
FISHING
FOOD
FOOTBALL
HIKING
INSIDER HOLLYWOOD
MANAGEMENT
OPERA
POETRY
QUANTUM UNIVERSE
HORSERACING
ROCK
RUGBY
SEX
SKIING
SOCIAL MEDIA
STAND-UP COMEDY
SURFING
TENNIS
UNIVERSITY
WINE
YOUR OWN BUSINESS

BLUFFERS.COM
@BLUFFERSGUIDE